Protected by God's Providence

The Book of Esther

Carolyn Culver

REGULAR BAPTIST PRESS
1300 North Meacham Road
Schaumburg, Illinois 60173-4806

Dedication

This study was written for and is dedicated to the precious ladies
who have joined me in Bible study on Sunday mornings at
Heritage Baptist Church, Clarks Summit, Pennsylvania, and
Calvary Baptist Church, Wisconsin Rapids, Wisconsin.
You have prompted growth in my life, and I am grateful for you.

All Scripture quotations are from the New King James Version of the Bible.
(© 1979, 1980, 1982 by Thomas Nelson, Inc. Used by permission. All rights
reserved.)

PROTECTED BY GOD'S PROVIDENCE: THE BOOK OF ESTHER
© 2007
Regular Baptist Press • Schaumburg, Illinois
www.regularbaptistpress.org • 1-800-727-4440
Printed in U.S.A.
All rights reserved
RBP5358 • ISBN: 978-0-87227-340-5

Contents

Preface

IN THE EARLY stages of preparing this study for a ladies' Sunday School class, I began to realize that the book of Esther has been perceived by some as romantic and Esther herself as privileged. However, rather than envying Esther for her beauty, selection as a queen, and position of influence, my heart broke for the pain she sustained as one who had not been taught to honor Jehovah God as her own.

The book of Esther stands as a precious reminder to me of how God works out His own purposes. Oftentimes I sense He is in front of me, beckoning me to follow Him. Other times, as in the story of Esther, He seems to direct from backstage, from behind a curtain, but very much in control. What unparalleled protection God's people have experienced— all because of God's providence.

Esther: A Script[1]

BECAUSE the book of Esther is a story with a beginning, middle, conclusion, plot, characters, theme, and events, we need to read it as a story. In fact this book, with its cast of a hero and heroine, a villain, drama, irony, humor, and suspense, lends itself to reading aloud.

In the following pages, the text of the book of Esther has been scripted into ten scenes, using a variety of narrators and other cast members to tell the story. A group can read the entire story from beginning to end with sixteen different roles; the group may also read one segment of the story with each lesson session.

God Rules—Even in Darkness
Esther 1:1–22

NARRATOR 1: [1]Now it came to pass in the days of Ahasuerus (this was the Ahasuerus who reigned over one hundred and twenty-seven provinces, from India to Ethiopia), [2]in those days when King Ahasuerus sat on the throne of his kingdom, which was in Shushan the citadel, [3]that in the third year of his reign he made a feast for all his officials and servants—the powers of Persia and Media, the nobles, and the princes of the provinces being before him—[4]when he showed the riches of his glorious kingdom and the splendor of his excellent majesty for many days, one hundred and eighty days in all.

NARRATOR 2: [5]And when these days were completed, the king made a feast lasting seven days for all the people who were present in Shushan the citadel, from great to small, in the court of the garden of the king's palace.

NARRATOR 3: [6]There were white and blue linen curtains fastened with cords of fine linen and purple on silver rods and marble pillars; and the couches were of gold and silver on a mosaic pavement of alabaster, turquoise, and white and black marble.

NARRATOR 1: [7]And they served drinks in golden vessels, each vessel being different from the other, with royal wine in abundance, according to the generosity of the king. [8]In accordance with the law, the drinking was not compulsory; for so the king had ordered all the officers of his household, that they should do according to each man's pleasure.

NARRATOR 2: [9]Queen Vashti also made a feast for the women in the royal palace which belonged to King Ahasuerus.

NARRATOR 3: [10]On the seventh day, when the heart of the king was merry with wine, he commanded Mehuman, Biztha, Harbona, Bigtha, Abagtha, Zethar, and Carcas, seven eunuchs who served in the presence of King Ahasuerus, [11]to bring Queen Vashti before the king, wearing her royal crown, in order to show her beauty to the people and the officials, for she was beautiful to behold.

NARRATORS 1 and 2: [12]But Queen Vashti refused to come at the king's command brought by his eunuchs; therefore the king was furious, and his anger burned within him.

NARRATOR 3: [13]Then the king said to the wise men who understood the times (for this was the king's manner toward all who knew law and justice, [14]those closest to him being Carshena, Shethar, Admatha, Tarshish, Meres, Marsena, and Memucan, the seven princes of Persia and Media, who had access to the king's presence, and who ranked highest in the kingdom):

KING: "What shall we do to Queen Vashti, according to law, because she did not obey the command of King Ahasuerus brought to her by the eunuchs?"

NARRATOR 1:   [16]And Memucan answered before the king and the princes:

MEMUCAN: "Queen Vashti has not only wronged the king, but also all the princes, and all the people who are in all the provinces of King Ahasuerus. [17]For the queen's behavior will become known to all women, so that they will despise their husbands in their eyes, when they report,   *oppression of women?*

ATTENDANT: King Ahasuerus commanded Queen Vashti to be brought in before him, but she did not come.

MEMUCAN: [18]This very day the noble ladies of Persia and Media will say to all the king's officials that they have heard of the behavior of the queen. Thus there will be excessive contempt and wrath. [19]If it pleases the king, let a royal decree go out from him, and let it be recorded in the laws of the Persians and the Medes, so that it will not be altered, that Vashti shall come no more before King Ahasuerus; and let the king give her royal position to another who is better than she. [20]When the king's decree which he will make is proclaimed throughout all his empire (for it is great), all wives will honor their husbands, both great and small."   *Biblical, but verses is not honoring Vashti*

NARRATOR 2:   [21]And the reply pleased the king and the princes, and the king did according to the word of Memucan.

NARRATOR 3:   [22]Then he sent letters to all the king's provinces, to each province in its own script, and to every people in their own language, that each man should be master in his own house, and speak in the language of his own people.

A Search for a Star
Esther 2:1–11

NARRATOR 1:   [1]After these things, when the wrath of King Ahasuerus subsided, he remembered Vashti, what she had done, and what had been decreed against her. [2]Then the king's servants who attended him said:

ATTENDANT 1:   "Let beautiful young virgins be sought for the king; [3]and
                 let the king appoint officers in all the provinces of his
                 kingdom, that they may gather all the beautiful young
                 virgins to Shushan the citadel, into the women's quarters,
                 under the custody of Hegai the king's eunuch, custodian of
                 the women.

ATTENDANT 2:   And let beauty preparations be given them. [4]Then let the
                 young woman who pleases the king be queen instead of
                 Vashti."

NARRATORS 1
    and 2:   This thing pleased the king, and he did so.

NARRATOR 3:   [5]In Shushan the citadel there was a certain Jew whose
                 name was Mordecai the son of Jair, the son of Shimei,
                 the son of Kish, a Benjamite. [6]Kish had been carried away
                 from Jerusalem with the captives who had been captured
                 with Jeconiah king of Judah, whom Nebuchadnezzar the
                 king of Babylon had carried away.

NARRATOR 1:   [7]And Mordecai had brought up Hadassah, that is, Esther, his
                 uncle's daughter, for she had neither father nor mother. The
                 young woman was lovely and beautiful. When her father and
                 mother died, Mordecai took her as his own daughter.

NARRATOR 2:   [8]So it was, when the king's command and decree were
                 heard, and when many young women were gathered at
                 Shushan the citadel, under the custody of Hegai, that
                 Esther also was taken to the king's palace, into the care of
                 Hegai the custodian of the women.

NARRATOR 3:   [9]Now the young woman pleased him, and she obtained
                 his favor; so he readily gave beauty preparations to her,
                 besides her allowance. Then seven choice maidservants
                 were provided for her from the king's palace, and he
                 moved her and her maidservants to the best place in the
                 house of the women.

NARRATOR 1:   [10]Esther had not revealed her people or family, for

Mordecai had charged her not to reveal it. [11]And every day Mordecai paced in front of the court of the women's quarters, to learn of Esther's welfare and what was happening to her.

Only God . . . Chooses a Star
Esther 2:12–23

NARRATOR 2:   [12]Each young woman's turn came to go in to King Ahasuerus after she had completed twelve months' preparation, according to the regulations for the women, for thus were the days of their preparation apportioned: six months with oil of myrrh, and six months with perfumes and preparations for beautifying women.

NARRATOR 3:   [13]Thus prepared, each young woman went to the king, and she was given whatever she desired to take with her from the women's quarters to the king's palace. [14]In the evening she went, and in the morning she returned to the second house of the women, to the custody of Shaashgaz, the king's eunuch who kept the concubines. She would not go in to the king again unless the king delighted in her and called for her by name.

NARRATOR 1:   [15]Now when the turn came for Esther the daughter of Abihail the uncle of Mordecai, who had taken her as his daughter, to go in to the king, she requested nothing but what Hegai the king's eunuch, the custodian of the women, advised.

NARRATORS 2 and 3:   And Esther obtained favor in the sight of all who saw her.

NARRATOR 1:   [16]So Esther was taken to King Ahasuerus, into his royal palace, in the tenth month, which is the month of Tebeth, in the seventh year of his reign.

NARRATORS 2
and 3:   [17]The king loved Esther more than all the other women,
            and she obtained grace and favor in his sight more than all
            the virgins; so he set the royal crown upon her head and
            made her queen instead of Vashti.

NARRATOR 1: [18]Then the king made a great feast, the Feast of Esther, for
            all his officials and servants; and he proclaimed a holiday in
            the provinces and gave gifts according to the generosity of a
            king.

NARRATOR 2: [19]When virgins were gathered together a second time,
            Mordecai sat within the king's gate. [20]Now Esther had not
            revealed her family and her people, just as Mordecai had
            charged her, for Esther obeyed the command of Mordecai
            as when she was brought up by him.

NARRATOR 3: [21]In those days, while Mordecai sat within the king's
            gate, two of the king's eunuchs, Bigthan and Teresh,
            doorkeepers, became furious and sought to lay hands on
            King Ahasuerus.

NARRATOR 1: [22]So the matter became known to Mordecai, who told
            Queen Esther, and Esther informed the king in Mordecai's
            name. [23]And when an inquiry was made into the matter, it
            was confirmed, and both were hanged on a gallows;

NARRATOR 2: and it was written in the book of the chronicles in the
            presence of the king.

Devising Destruction
Esther 3:1–15

NARRATOR 1: [1]After these things King Ahasuerus promoted Haman, the
            son of Hammedatha the Agagite, and advanced him and
            set his seat above all the princes who were with him. [2]And
            all the king's servants who were within the king's gate
            bowed and paid homage to Haman, for so the king had
            commanded concerning him.

NARRATOR 2: But Mordecai would not bow or pay homage. [3]Then the king's servants who were within the king's gate said to Mordecai,

OFFICIAL: "Why do you transgress the king's command?"

NARRATOR 3: [4]Now it happened, when they spoke to him daily and he would not listen to them, that they told it to Haman, to see whether Mordecai's words would stand; for Mordecai had told them that he was a Jew.

NARRATOR 1: [5]When Haman saw that Mordecai did not bow or pay him homage, Haman was filled with wrath. [6]But he disdained to lay hands on Mordecai alone, for they had told him of the people of Mordecai.

NARRATOR 2: Instead, Haman sought to destroy all the Jews who were throughout the whole kingdom of Ahasuerus—the people of Mordecai.

NARRATOR 3: [7]In the first month, which is the month of Nisan, in the twelfth year of King Ahasuerus, they cast Pur (that is, the lot), before Haman to determine the day and the month, until it fell on the twelfth month, which is the month of Adar. [8]Then Haman said to King Ahasuerus,

HAMAN: "There is a certain people scattered and dispersed among the people in all the provinces of your kingdom; their laws are different from all other people's, and they do not keep the king's laws. Therefore it is not fitting for the king to let them remain. [9]If it pleases the king, let a decree be written that they be destroyed, and I will pay ten thousand talents of silver into the hands of those who do the work, to bring it into the king's treasuries."

NARRATOR 1: [10]So the king took his signet ring from his hand and gave it to Haman, the son of Hammedatha the Agagite, the enemy of the Jews. [11]And the king said to Haman,

KING: "The money and the people are given to you, to do with them as seems good to you."

NARRATOR 2:   [12]Then the king's scribes were called on the thirteenth day of the first month, and a decree was written according to all that Haman commanded—to the king's satraps, to the governors who were over each province, to the officials of all people, to every province according to its script, and to every people in their language.

NARRATOR 3:   In the name of King Ahasuerus it was written, and sealed with the king's signet ring. [13]And the letters were sent by couriers into all the king's provinces, to destroy, to kill, and to annihilate all the Jews, both young and old, little children and women, in one day, on the thirteenth day of the twelfth month, which is the month of Adar, and to plunder their possessions.

NARRATOR 1:   [14]A copy of the document was to be issued as law in every province, being published for all people, that they should be ready for that day. [15]The couriers went out, hastened by the king's command; and the decree was proclaimed in Shushan the citadel.

NARRATORS 2
    and 3:   So the king and Haman sat down to drink, but the city of Shushan was perplexed.

Choosing Commitment with Courage
Esther 4:1–17

NARRATOR 1:   [1]When Mordecai learned all that had happened, he tore his clothes and put on sackcloth and ashes, and went out into the midst of the city. He cried out with a loud and bitter cry. [2]He went as far as the front of the king's gate, for no one might enter the king's gate clothed with sackcloth.

NARRATOR 2:   [3]And in every province where the king's command and decree arrived, there was great mourning among the Jews, with fasting, weeping, and wailing; and many lay in sackcloth and ashes.

NARRATOR 3:   [4]So Esther's maids and eunuchs came and told her, and the queen was deeply distressed. Then she sent garments to clothe Mordecai and take his sackcloth away from him, but he would not accept them.

NARRATOR 1:   [5]Then Esther called Hathach, one of the king's eunuchs whom he had appointed to attend her, and she gave him a command concerning Mordecai, to learn what and why this was.

NARRATOR 2:   [6]So Hathach went out to Mordecai in the city square that was in front of the king's gate.

NARRATOR 3:   [7]And Mordecai told him all that had happened to him, and the sum of money that Haman had promised to pay into the king's treasuries to destroy the Jews. [8]He also gave him a copy of the written decree for their destruction, which was given at Shushan, that he might show it to Esther and explain it to her, and that he might command her to go in to the king to make supplication to him and plead before him for her people.

NARRATOR 1:   [9]So Hathach returned and told Esther the words of Mordecai. [10]Then Esther spoke to Hathach, and gave him a command for Mordecai:

ESTHER: [11]"All the king's servants and the people of the king's provinces know that any man or woman who goes into the inner court to the king, who has not been called, he has but one law: put all to death, except the one to whom the king holds out the golden scepter, that he may live. Yet I myself have not been called to go in to the king these thirty days."

NARRATOR 1:   [12]So they told Mordecai Esther's words. [13]And Mordecai told them to answer Esther:

MORDECAI: "Do not think in your heart that you will escape in the king's palace any more than all the other Jews. [14]For if you remain completely silent at this time, relief and deliverance will

NARRATOR 2: arise for the Jews from another place, but you and your father's house will perish. Yet who knows whether you have come to the kingdom for such a time as this?"

NARRATOR 2: [15]Then Esther told them to reply to Mordecai:

ESTHER: [16]"Go, gather all the Jews who are present in Shushan, and fast for me; neither eat nor drink for three days, night or day. My maids and I will fast likewise. And so I will go to the king, which is against the law; and if I perish, I perish!"

NARRATOR 3: [17]So Mordecai went his way and did according to all that Esther commanded him.

Too Late to Turn Back
Esther 5:1–14

NARRATOR 1: [1]Now it happened on the third day that Esther put on her royal robes and stood in the inner court of the king's palace, across from the king's house, while the king sat on his royal throne in the royal house, facing the entrance of the house.

NARRATOR 2: [2]So it was, when the king saw Queen Esther standing in the court, that she found favor in his sight, and the king held out to Esther the golden scepter that was in his hand. Then Esther went near and touched the top of the scepter. [3]And the king said to her,

KING: "What do you wish, Queen Esther? What is your request? It shall be given to you—up to half the kingdom!"

NARRATOR 3: [4]So Esther answered,

ESTHER: "If it pleases the king, let the king and Haman come today to the banquet that I have prepared for him."

NARRATOR 1: [5]Then the king said,

KING: "Bring Haman quickly, that he may do as Esther has said."

NARRATOR 2: So the king and Haman went to the banquet that Esther had prepared. [6]At the banquet of wine the king said to Esther,

KING: "What is your petition? It shall be granted you. What is your request, up to half the kingdom? It shall be done!"

NARRATOR 3: [7]Then Esther answered and said,

ESTHER: "My petition and request is this: [8]If I have found favor in the sight of the king, and if it pleases the king to grant my petition and fulfill my request, then let the king and Haman come to the banquet which I will prepare for them, and tomorrow I will do as the king has said."

NARRATOR 1: [9]So Haman went out that day joyful and with a glad heart; but when Haman saw Mordecai in the king's gate, and that he did not stand or tremble before him, he was filled with indignation against Mordecai. [10]Nevertheless Haman restrained himself and went home, and he sent and called for his friends and his wife Zeresh.

NARRATOR 2: [11]Then Haman told them of his great riches, the multitude of his children, everything in which the king had promoted him, and how he had advanced him above the officials and servants of the king. [12]Moreover Haman said,

HAMAN: "Besides, Queen Esther invited no one but me to come in with the king to the banquet that she prepared; and tomorrow I am again invited by her, along with the king. [13]Yet all this avails me nothing, so long as I see Mordecai the Jew sitting at the king's gate."

NARRATOR 3: [14]Then his wife Zeresh and all his friends said to him, "Let a gallows be made, fifty cubits high, and in the morning suggest to the king that Mordecai be hanged on it; then go merrily with the king to the banquet."

NARRATOR 1: And the thing pleased Haman; so he had the gallows made.

From Sleeplessness to Celebration
Esther 6:1–14

NARRATOR 2:   [1]That night the king could not sleep. So one was
commanded to bring the book of the records of the
chronicles; and they were read before the king. [2]And it
was found written that Mordecai had told of Bigthana and
Teresh, two of the king's eunuchs, the doorkeepers who
had sought to lay hands on King Ahasuerus. [3]Then the king
said,

KING: "What honor or dignity has been bestowed on Mordecai
for this?"

NARRATOR 3:   And the king's servants who attended him said,

SERVANT: "Nothing has been done for him."

NARRATOR 1:   [4]So the king said,

KING: "Who is in the court?"

NARRATOR 2:   Now Haman had just entered the outer court of the king's
palace to suggest that the king hang Mordecai on the
gallows that he had prepared for him. [5]The king's servants
said to him,

SERVANT: "Haman is there, standing in the court."

NARRATOR 3:   And the king said,

KING: "Let him come in."

NARRATOR 1:   [6]So Haman came in, and the king asked him,

KING: "What shall be done for the man whom the king delights
to honor?"

NARRATOR 2:   Now Haman thought in his heart,

HAMAN
(*to himself*):   "Whom would the king delight to honor more than me?"

NARRATOR 3:   [7]And Haman answered the king,

HAMAN: "For the man whom the king delights to honor, [8]let a royal
robe be brought which the king has worn, and a horse on
which the king has ridden, which has a royal crest placed

on its head. ⁹Then let this robe and horse be delivered to the hand of one of the king's most noble princes, that he may array the man whom the king delights to honor. Then parade him on horseback through the city square, and proclaim before him: 'Thus shall it be done to the man whom the king delights to honor!'"

NARRATOR 1: ¹⁰Then the king said to Haman,

KING: "Hurry, take the robe and the horse, as you have suggested, and do so for Mordecai the Jew who sits within the king's gate! Leave nothing undone of all that you have spoken."

NARRATOR 2: ¹¹So Haman took the robe and the horse, arrayed Mordecai and led him on horseback through the city square, and proclaimed before him,

HAMAN: "Thus shall it be done to the man whom the king delights to honor!"

NARRATOR 3: ¹²Afterward Mordecai went back to the king's gate. But Haman hurried to his house, mourning and with his head covered. ¹³When Haman told his wife Zeresh and all his friends everything that had happened to him, his wise men and his wife Zeresh said to him,

ZERESH: "If Mordecai, before whom you have begun to fall, is of Jewish descent, you will not prevail against him but will surely fall before him."

NARRATOR 1: ¹⁴While they were still talking with him, the king's eunuchs came, and hastened to bring Haman to the banquet which Esther had prepared.

More Surprises as the Day Continues
Esther 7:1–10

NARRATOR 2: ¹So the king and Haman went to dine with Queen Esther. ²And on the second day, at the banquet of wine, the king again said to Esther,

KING: "What is your petition, Queen Esther? It shall be granted
             you. And what is your request, up to half the kingdom? It
             shall be done!"

NARRATOR 3: [3]Then Queen Esther answered and said,

ESTHER: "If I have found favor in your sight, O king, and if it
             pleases the king, let my life be given me at my petition,
             and my people at my request. [4]For we have been sold,
             my people and I, to be destroyed, to be killed, and to be
             annihilated. Had we been sold as male and female slaves,
             I would have held my tongue, although the enemy could
             never compensate for the king's loss."

NARRATOR 1: [5]So King Ahasuerus answered and said to Queen Esther,

KING: "Who is he, and where is he, who would dare presume in
             his heart to do such a thing?"

NARRATOR 1: [6]And Esther said,

ESTHER: "The adversary and enemy is this wicked Haman!"

NARRATOR 2: So Haman was terrified before the king and queen.

NARRATOR 3: [7]Then the king arose in his wrath from the banquet of
             wine and went into the palace garden; but Haman stood
             before Queen Esther, pleading for his life, for he saw
             that evil was determined against him by the king. [8]When
             the king returned from the palace garden to the place of
             the banquet of wine, Haman had fallen across the couch
             where Esther was. Then the king said,

KING: "Will he also assault the queen while I am in the house?"

NARRATOR 1: As the word left the king's mouth, they covered Haman's
             face. [9]Now Harbonah, one of the eunuchs, said to the king,

HARBONAH: "Look! The gallows, fifty cubits high, which Haman made
             for Mordecai, who spoke good on the king's behalf, is
             standing at the house of Haman."

NARRATOR 1: Then the king said,

KING: "Hang him on it!"

NARRATORS 2
and 3:   [10]So they hanged Haman on the gallows that he had
             prepared for Mordecai. Then the king's wrath subsided.

Wait! What about the Decree?
Esther 8:1–17

NARRATOR 1:   [1]On that day King Ahasuerus gave Queen Esther the house
              of Haman, the enemy of the Jews. And Mordecai came
              before the king, for Esther had told how he was related to
              her.

NARRATOR 2:   [2]So the king took off his signet ring, which he had
              taken from Haman, and gave it to Mordecai; and Esther
              appointed Mordecai over the house of Haman.

NARRATOR 3:   [3]Now Esther spoke again to the king, fell down at his feet,
              and implored him with tears to counteract the evil of
              Haman the Agagite, and the scheme which he had devised
              against the Jews. [4]And the king held out the golden scepter
              toward Esther. So Esther arose and stood before the king,
              [5]and said,

ESTHER: "If it pleases the king, and if I have found favor in his sight
              and the thing seems right to the king and I am pleasing
              in his eyes, let it be written to revoke the letters devised
              by Haman, the son of Hammedatha the Agagite, which
              he wrote to annihilate the Jews who are in all the king's
              provinces. [6]For how can I endure to see the evil that
              will come to my people? Or how can I endure to see the
              destruction of my countrymen?"

NARRATOR 1:   [7]Then King Ahasuerus said to Queen Esther and Mordecai
              the Jew,

KING: "Indeed, I have given Esther the house of Haman, and
              they have hanged him on the gallows because he tried to
              lay his hand on the Jews. [8]You yourselves write a decree

concerning the Jews, as you please, in the king's name, and seal it with the king's signet ring; for whatever is written in the king's name and sealed with the king's signet ring no one can revoke."

NARRATOR 2: [9]So the king's scribes were called at that time, in the third month, which is the month of Sivan, on the twenty-third day; and it was written, according to all that Mordecai commanded, to the Jews, the satraps, the governors, and the princes of the provinces from India to Ethiopia, one hundred and twenty-seven provinces in all, to every province in its own script, to every people in their own language, and to the Jews in their own script and language. [10]And he wrote in the name of King Ahasuerus, sealed it with the king's signet ring, and sent letters by couriers on horseback, riding on royal horses bred from swift steeds.

NARRATOR 3: [11]By these letters the king permitted the Jews who were in every city to gather together and protect their lives—to destroy, kill, and annihilate all the forces of any people or province that would assault them, both little children and women, and to plunder their possessions, [12]on one day in all the provinces of King Ahasuerus, on the thirteenth day of the twelfth month, which is the month of Adar.

NARRATOR 1: [13]A copy of the document was to be issued as a decree in every province and published for all people, so that the Jews would be ready on that day to avenge themselves on their enemies. [14]The couriers who rode on royal horses went out, hastened and pressed on by the king's command. And the decree was issued in Shushan the citadel.

NARRATOR 2: [15]So Mordecai went out from the presence of the king in royal apparel of blue and white, with a great crown of gold and a garment of fine linen and purple; and the city of Shushan rejoiced and was glad.

NARRATOR 3: [16]The Jews had light and gladness, joy and honor. [17]And in every province and city, wherever the king's command and decree came, the Jews had joy and gladness, a feast and a holiday. Then many of the people of the land became Jews, because fear of the Jews fell upon them.

From Fighting to Feasting—Let's Celebrate!
Esther 9:1—10:3

NARRATOR 1:   [1]Now in the twelfth month, that is, the month of Adar, on the thirteenth day, the time came for the king's command and his decree to be executed. On the day that the enemies of the Jews had hoped to overpower them, the opposite occurred, in that the Jews themselves overpowered those who hated them.

NARRATOR 2:   [2]The Jews gathered together in their cities throughout all the provinces of King Ahasuerus to lay hands on those who sought their harm. And no one could withstand them, because fear of them fell upon all people.

NARRATOR 3:   [3]And all the officials of the provinces, the satraps, the governors, and all those doing the king's work, helped the Jews, because the fear of Mordecai fell upon them. [4]For Mordecai was great in the king's palace, and his fame spread throughout all the provinces; for this man Mordecai became increasingly prominent. [5]Thus the Jews defeated all their enemies with the stroke of the sword, with slaughter and destruction, and did what they pleased with those who hated them.

NARRATOR 1:   [6]And in Shushan the citadel the Jews killed and destroyed five hundred men. [7]Also Parshandatha, Dalphon, Aspatha, [8]Poratha, Adalia, Aridatha, [9]Parmashta, Arisai, Aridai, and Vajezatha— [10]the ten sons of Haman the son of Hammedatha, the enemy of the Jews—they killed; but they did not lay a hand on the plunder.

NARRATOR 2:   [11]On that day the number of those who were killed in
               Shushan the citadel was brought to the king. [12]And the
               king said to Queen Esther,

KING: "The Jews have killed and destroyed five hundred men in
               Shushan the citadel, and the ten sons of Haman. What have
               they done in the rest of the king's provinces? Now what is
               your petition? It shall be granted to you. Or what is your
               further request? It shall be done."

NARRATOR 3:   [13]Then Esther said,

ESTHER: "If it pleases the king, let it be granted to the Jews who are in
               Shushan to do again tomorrow according to today's decree, and
               let Haman's ten sons be hanged on the gallows."

NARRATOR 1:   [14]So the king commanded this to be done; the decree was
               issued in Shushan, and they hanged Haman's ten sons.
               [15]And the Jews who were in Shushan gathered together
               again on the fourteenth day of the month of Adar and
               killed three hundred men at Shushan; but they did not lay
               a hand on the plunder.

NARRATOR 2:   [16]The remainder of the Jews in the king's provinces
               gathered together and protected their lives, had rest from
               their enemies, and killed seventy-five thousand of their
               enemies; but they did not lay a hand on the plunder. [17]This
               was on the thirteenth day of the month of Adar. And on the
               fourteenth of the month they rested and made it a day of
               feasting and gladness.

NARRATOR 3:   [18]But the Jews who were at Shushan assembled together
               on the thirteenth day, as well as on the fourteenth; and on
               the fifteenth of the month they rested, and made it a day of
               feasting and gladness.

NARRATOR 1:   [19]Therefore the Jews of the villages who dwelt in the
               unwalled towns celebrated the fourteenth day of the month
               of Adar with gladness and feasting, as a holiday, and for
               sending presents to one another.

NARRATOR 2:   [20]And Mordecai wrote these things and sent letters to
                 all the Jews, near and far, who were in all the provinces
                 of King Ahasuerus, [21]to establish among them that they
                 should celebrate yearly the fourteenth and fifteenth days of
                 the month of Adar, [22]as the days on which the Jews had rest
                 from their enemies, as the month which was turned from
                 sorrow to joy for them, and from mourning to a holiday;
                 that they should make them days of feasting and joy, of
                 sending presents to one another and gifts to the poor.

NARRATOR 3:   [23]So the Jews accepted the custom which they had begun,
                 as Mordecai had written to them, [24]because Haman, the
                 son of Hammedatha the Agagite, the enemy of all the
                 Jews, had plotted against the Jews to annihilate them,
                 and had cast Pur (that is, the lot), to consume them and
                 destroy them; [25]but when Esther came before the king, he
                 commanded by letter that this wicked plot which Haman
                 had devised against the Jews should return on his own
                 head, and that he and his sons should be hanged on the
                 gallows.

NARRATOR 1:   [26]So they called these days Purim, after the name Pur.

NARRATOR 2:   Therefore, because of all the words of this letter, what they
                 had seen concerning this matter, and what had happened
                 to them, [27]the Jews established and imposed it upon
                 themselves and their descendants and all who would join
                 them, that without fail they should celebrate these two
                 days every year, according to the written instructions and
                 according to the prescribed time, [28]that these days should
                 be remembered and kept throughout every generation,
                 every family, every province, and every city, that these days
                 of Purim should not fail to be observed among the Jews,
                 and that the memory of them should not perish among
                 their descendants.

NARRATOR 3:   [29]Then Queen Esther, the daughter of Abihail, with

Mordecai the Jew, wrote with full authority to confirm this second letter about Purim.

NARRATOR 1:   [30]And Mordecai sent letters to all the Jews, to the one hundred and twenty-seven provinces of the kingdom of Ahasuerus, with words of peace and truth, [31]to confirm these days of Purim at their appointed time, as Mordecai the Jew and Queen Esther had prescribed for them, and as they had decreed for themselves and their descendants concerning matters of their fasting and lamenting. [32]So the decree of Esther confirmed these matters of Purim, and it was written in the book.

NARRATOR 2:   [1]And King Ahasuerus imposed tribute on the land and on the islands of the sea. [2]Now all the acts of his power and his might, and the account of the greatness of Mordecai, to which the king advanced him, are they not written in the book of the chronicles of the kings of Media and Persia?

NARRATOR 3:   [3]For Mordecai the Jew was second to King Ahasuerus, and was great among the Jews and well received by the multitude of his brethren, seeking the good of his people and speaking peace to all his countrymen.

Notes
1. New King James Version (Nashville: Thomas Nelson, 1982).

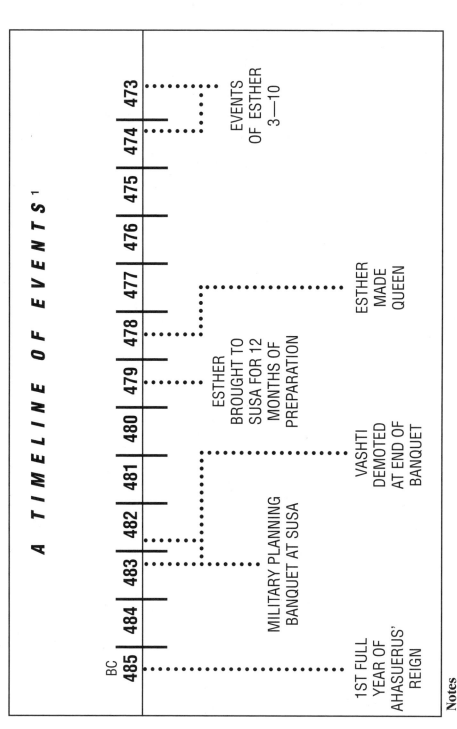

A TIMELINE OF EVENTS [1]

| BC 485 | 484 | 483 | 482 | 481 | 480 | 479 | 478 | 477 | 476 | 475 | 474 | 473 |

1ST FULL
YEAR OF
AHASUERUS'
REIGN

MILITARY PLANNING
BANQUET AT SUSA

VASHTI
DEMOTED
AT END OF
BANQUET

ESTHER
BROUGHT TO
SUSA FOR 12
MONTHS OF
PREPARATION

ESTHER
MADE
QUEEN

EVENTS
OF ESTHER
3—10

Notes

1. John C. Whitcomb, *Esther: Triumph of God's Sovereignty* (Chicago: Moody Bible Institute, 1979), 34, 35.

1

God Rules—Even in Darkness

"And we know that all things work together for good to those who love God, to those who are the called according to His purpose" (Romans 8:28).

DO YOU sometimes think it would be easier to hear and believe God if you could actually see Him face to face? Do you ever doubt His protection and work in your life? Since He does not give us tangible appearances and audible messages, can you be certain He has not forgotten you when times are difficult? Imagine yourself living as a displaced captive—assurance of God's presence and protection could be difficult to grasp and maintain in such circumstances.

Even when life seems very dark, God continues to work and to orchestrate the events and circumstances of our lives. God is the sovereign controller of our lives. Although no name of God is mentioned in the book of Esther, His providence, protection, and preservation are obvious.

When God made His covenant with the nation Israel in the days of Moses, He promised to bless the nation if its people obeyed Him, but to send them into exile if they were not loyal (Deuteronomy 28). Many years before the birth of Esther, sin in the lives of the Jewish people resulted in their captivity. Over and over, God's people had rebelled against Him. He had sent prophets to warn them, but they continued in their disobedience. As the book of Esther opens, many Jews remained scattered in pagan lands.

Esther was a young Jewish woman living under the rule of Persia, the most powerful government in the world. The king was Ahasuerus (also known as Xerxes), a dictator with a beautiful wife, Queen Vashti.

This story that happened 2,500 years ago contains a hero and heroine, a villain, drama, irony, humor, and suspense. God used a husband-wife conflict, a beauty contest, conspiracy, murder, triumph, and revenge to overcome seemingly impossible circumstances.

As we study this intriguing book of inspired Scripture, we will learn much of God and the way He continues to work in human lives. We will see Romans 8:28 illustrated repeatedly as God works all things according to His will and for the good of His people. We will be convinced that He remains in control of circumstances and events today. We will realize anew that He disciplines His people, but He never abandons them. What an awesome God!

> What a mighty God we serve,
> What a mighty God we serve,
> Angels bow before Him, heaven and earth adore Him.
> What a mighty God we serve.[1]

Because the book of Esther is a story with a beginning, middle, conclusion, plot, characters, theme, and events, we need to read it as a story. Read through the "Getting the Big Picture" questions that follow, then read the entire book of Esther, recording your initial observations of God's providence.

When we speak of God's providence, we mean that God, in some invisible and inscrutable way, governs all creatures, actions, and circumstances through the normal and the ordinary course of human life, without the intervention of the miraculous.[2]

Getting the Big Picture

1. Because God is in control, there are no coincidences nor is there such a thing as luck. Even though God is unseen and unmentioned, there are many evidences of His hand at work throughout the book of Esther.

Look for some of the circumstances that seem to be coincidences but actually evidence the providential control of God. A few examples are *pg. 116* already cited.

- King calls Vashti out during feast (not customary)

- Queen Vashti refused to obey the king's summons.

- over reaction & getting rid of Vashti (divorce)

- Search whole kingdom — does not say to disinclude Jewish women, Esther not of royal blood

- Esther was beautiful

- Esther's heritage was unknown (usually spreads fast)

- Hegai, the servant responsible for the king's harem, was partial toward Esther.

- King choose Esther as Queen

- Mordecai learns of plot to kill the King

- villian← Haman was elevated w/ great authority

- Mordecai's deed of foiling a murder plot was recorded but not rewarded.

- Date of execution of Jews 11 months after date of decree — if next day Esther would have no time to invite to dinner
-

2. There are no references to God, prayer, or worship in the account concerning Esther, but fasting does occur. As you read through the book of Esther, find two occasions of fasting. Note the verse reference and include the when, the whom, and the why of the fasting.

(a)

(b)

3. Celebrations were held as feasts. As you read through Esther, note each feast, its host or hostess, and its purpose. The first feast is identified for you.

(a) 1:3: The king was the host; the feast lasted seven days; its purposes were to show the king's power and to launch a military campaign.

(b) Feast of Esther, held by the King as a celebration of the new queen

(c)

(d)

(e)

4. Record questions that come to mind as you read through the book. An example is included.

- Why don't we know that the Jews prayed when they fasted?

- Why does ~~Esther~~ the King not mention Jews? — God's hand ↳when looking for a new wife

-

-

-

Who wrote the book of Esther? Most likely, it was written by a Jew who also lived under Persian rule, perhaps even an eyewitness of the book's events. It probably was written to be read aloud as part of the ceremony at the Feast of Purim. This annual feast (which will be discussed as we study Esther chapter 9) is a yearly reminder of God's faithfulness on behalf of His people.

Make It Personal

5. What are several occasions when you have cited or heard someone else cite Romans 8:28 in reference to difficult circumstances?

- Maddie — realized it was for the good of God's Kingdom, not just her own. Helped her to endure hurt.
- People who have gone through loss to have used this verse to remember God's provision & purpose

-

6. Review the true story of your own life.

(a) In two or three sentences tell the who, when, and where of the beginning of your life.

My parents & their families; 1996, July, 7 months after they were married; Baltimore, non-Christian home

(b) Who do you recognize as "main characters" in your life so far?

My parents, Sierra, Lacey, Jackie, Ashley, Tracy, Summer Mission people, Annie, Caroline

(c) What has been one significant event in your life for each decade
you have lived, and what specific people were present in your life
during those events?

0 - 10   saved @ VBS (my sister)

10 - 20   Cru & Summer Mission (Annie, Caroline, SM people, Steph)

Draw a timeline from the year of your birth to the present. List significant people or significant events in your life from birth to today. You will find a timeline of events in the book of Esther on page 27.

Notes

1. Writer of words and music unknown.

2. Karen H. Jobes, *The NIV Application Commentary: Esther* (Grand Rapids: Zondervan, 1999), 43.

2

Punished without Pardon

ESTHER 1

*"Let us hold fast the confession of our hope without waver-
ing, for He who promised is faithful" (Hebrews 10:23).*

SOMETIMES we find ourselves in a no-win situation. No matter what we decide or how we act, we will not be able to prevent being blamed and perceived as guilty. As the wife of one in leadership, Queen Vashti was expected to be an example to all other women in the kingdom. Her disobedience to the king was seen by his advisers as a wrong against all of the people. Her position of leadership was so influential that the male leaders considered her to be the primary example and influence to the other women.

A King's Business

1. Read Esther 1:1–11. What was King Ahasuerus doing when the book of Esther begins (1:1–4)?

Feasting with officials.

2. When the king hosted a feast after that long planning meeting ended (1:5–8), what was apparently his principal activity (vv. 7, 8)?

Drinking for pleasure after planning kad

3. What did Queen Vashti do while the king was hosting his feast (1:9)?

Own feast w/ women, according to custom.

4. What entertainment did the king devise for himself and his guests (1:10, 11)?

Vashti's beauty

A Queen Is Tested

5. Read Esther 1:10–12. How did Vashti handle the king's summons?

She ~~den~~. went against him. It was a moral dilemma for her b/c it was against custom

6. Would you have handled this situation as Vashti did? Explain.

Probably, I am strong-willed and would not let someone else influence me to go against societal and personal morals.

In other historical literature, King Ahasuerus has been portrayed as a bold, ambitious, handsome, and self-indulgent man who could control everything except himself. He seemed to be an inconsistent ruler, a slave to alcohol, anger, extreme actions, and revenge. J. G. McConville calls Ahasuerus the "unacceptable face of human power."[1] It seems that an alliance with him would pose both threat and uncertainty to the ally.

At the feast of Esther 1:3, the king had called his military officials together over a six-month period for the purpose of planning war. At the conclusion of the session, he hosted a huge celebration. This probably was held as a public outdoor buffet in the garden areas surrounding the palace.

Persian law dictated that guests were to take a drink every time the king did. Known as a heavy drinker, the king waived this rule for those unable to keep up with him. In his drunken state, Vashti's husband decided to parade his queen and her physical beauty in front of his drunken guests so they might gaze upon her and envy him. He probably wanted her to perform some kind of showy walk with her crown and with less-than-modest attire.

No doubt this decision was prompted by drunkenness and pride, but it violated the Persian law that prohibited any man but the king from looking at the queen without her veil. The king sent word for Vashti to do something that would bring great dishonor to her husband as well as to her. She found herself in a no-win situation.

> [The king] would be requesting Vashti to do something beneath her station and demeaning to her royal personage. Exposing her to the gaze of the entire citadel population would be a far greater humiliation than not bowing to an honored official, but would be a similar violation of protocol.[2]

We know very little about Vashti. Physically, she was quite beautiful. As a mother, she was either still pregnant with Artaxerxes, or she was nursing him as an infant. We also know that she bravely refused to be part of a scandal and knew that the consequences of such public disobedience would be harsh.

Make It Personal

7. Consider some of the following passages as you answer the next few questions: 2 Timothy 2:22–26; Hebrews 10:23–25; James 3:13–18; 1 Peter 2:13—3:17; 4:12–16; 5:6–11.

(a) Is there a man in your circle (husband, father, brother, boss, neighbor) who shows traits like those of Ahasuerus?

(b) According to any of the Scriptures listed with question 7, what is your responsibility toward anyone that you named above?

gentle, humble, submissive

follow him, but (in God)

When we think about Ahasuerus—his priorities of riches, pleasure, and power, the way he made decisions by relying on those around him and making impetuous decisions that he later regretted—we do not see him as a positive role model. *we need to think seriously*

8. What do your personal priorities and decision-making principles say about you?

(a) How serious is your commitment to seek God's will and direction?

(b) Do you truly seek God's will and His direction for your decisions? If so, what counsel would you give to other women to help them set right priorities and make good decisions?

(c) If not, what does God want to change in your life?

9. Vashti paid a great price to retain her integrity. Recall a test of your own integrity.

    (a) What was at issue that time when you knew that doing right would be costly?

    (b) What moved you to act as you did in that situation?

    (c) What has been the long-term outcome of this test of your integrity?

10. What are some common tests of personal integrity?

11. What price are you prepared to pay to pass the next integrity test?

A Question of Control

Think about the small measure of control Ahasuerus actually had. Even though he reigned over 127 provinces and lived in enviable luxury, he possessed very little control over the events around him. God's providence continues to be seen in what appears to be normal circumstances. Ironically, the king was "consumed with power yet powerless as sovereign events unfold."[3]

A Dramatic Decree

12. According to Esther 1:13–22 what decree was made (v. 19)?

13. What fear prompted this decree (vv. 17, 18)?

14. What outcome was desired from this decree (vv. 20, 22)?

The advisors to Ahasuerus exaggerated the importance of Queen Vashti's refusal of the king's summons and warned him that her refusal would become a standard for all other women. These men feared they would lose control of their own wives. They prompted a decree that they thought would mandate honor and respect for husbands.

The recommended decree was extreme. Do you see God's hand at work in it? How?

It seems ironic and comical that men with so much worldly power would be ruled by fear of a national uprising because of the response of one woman. At the same time, this interaction between men and a woman foreshadows the way a young Jewish woman will rise above two powerful Persian men for the sake of an entire people group. The drama continues to build as a less-than-attractive monarch and a power-hungry administration make seemingly arbitrary decisions that affect individual lives and an entire nation.

There are many good and bad examples around us in the media and in everyday life. Those of us who desire our lives to shine as good testimonies need to remember that God wants to use each of us as a right example to other women.

Make It Personal

15. What is one area of character and behavior in which you know God wants to use you to influence others?

16. Before whom are you living as an example of God's standards of morality and appropriate conduct?

17. Read Hebrews 10:23, a key verse for this lesson. How might the counsel of this verse guide a woman who feels trapped in a Vashti-like situation?

Notes

1. J.G. McConville, *Ezra, Nehemiah, and Esther* (Philadelphia: The Westminster Press, 1985), 156.

2. John H. Walton, Victor H. Matthews, and Mark W. Chavalas, *The IVP Bible Background Commentary: Old Testament* (Downers Grove, IL: InterVarsity Press, 2000), 485.

3. Mervin Breneman, *The New American Commentary: Ezra, Nehemiah, Esther* (Nashville: Broadman and Holman Publishers, 1993), 323.

3

A Search for a Star

ESTHER 2:1–11

"For I know the thoughts that I think toward you, says the
Lord, thoughts of peace and not of evil, to give you a future
and a hope. . . . I will be found by you, says the Lord, and
I will bring you back from your captivity; I will gather
you from all the nations and from all the places where I
have driven you, says the Lord, and I will bring you to the
place from which I cause you to be carried away captive"
(Jeremiah 29:11, 14).

THE DAY ahead of you is not a coincidence; it will not just happen according to chance. The steps of your life are ordered by the Lord, and He weaves all of the experiences together to work them for your benefit.

It was not a coincidence that Ahasuerus called for his lovely queen, Vashti, who chose to disobey the king with the consequence that her royal life as she had known it ended. Another lovely young woman, Esther, had no idea that God was at work preparing a vacant seat for a new queen.

About four years passed between the dismissal of Vashti and the events of the beginning of chapter 2. During this time, King Ahasuerus and the Persian troops invaded Greece and returned home defeated and humiliated. Vashti was not present at this homecoming to welcome the king. Her absence, coupled with military defeat, must have provoked personal depression (2:1).

The king's servants were legally unable to restore Vashti as queen, so they deviated from the custom of the land and presented a plan for finding a new queen.

The Beauty Contest

1. Read Esther 2:2–4.

(a) Where did the idea for a new queen originate (v. 2; see also 1:12–21)?

The King's servants

(b) What were the specific elements in this plan (2:3, 4)?

Virgins, from land, not royals

Until now, only women from certain royal families had been eligible to marry a royal personage. This kingdom-wide search provided for any young woman to be selected. Do you see the work of God's hand in this?

Officers were appointed to gather women to the citadel, where they would be groomed for the king's choice. "Fathers apparently did not voluntarily present their daughters as evidenced by the king's appointment of officials to search for the candidates."[1]

> Little imagination is needed to appreciate the horror caused
> by the round-up of these girls, whose fate it was to be
> carried away from their homes to be secluded for life as the
> king's concubines. What a liability to be beautiful![2]

This compulsory beauty contest was not an exciting, romantic opportunity. The virgins who were taken to the palace were guaranteed a life of isolation and frustration. These beautiful young women and their families must have experienced much heartache and suffering by the plan to find a new queen. Undoubtedly, family plans were disrupted and engagements broken.

Living in the harem, the young women would be unable to see their families, to resume previous courtships, to marry another man, or to have

children. In most cases, they would spend only one night with the royal
husband, lose virginity, and never be called again. They would spend the
rest of their lives in seclusion in the house of the concubines and be de-
nied the privileges of an intimate relationship with a husband and the joys
of rearing children. This was not an opportunity to be envied!

2. Read Esther 2:5–8.

(a) A Jewish man is introduced into the account at this point. What is
his name, and where was he living in the Persian Empire (vv.
5, 6)?

(b) How did this Jew come to be living in this city rather than in the
homeland of Israel (v. 6)?

(c) A young woman is introduced into the story in verse 7. What two
names did she have?

(d) What was the connection between this young woman and the
Jewish man (v. 7)?

(e) In what city was this young woman residing when the decree of
Esther 2:3 and 4 was delivered (vv. 5–7)?

(f) How did that decree impact this young woman's life (vv. 7, 8)?

3. What might have been the benefits of already being a resident of the king's city?

Make It Personal

4. Recall a time when you feared that God had forgotten you. What circumstances contributed to that sense of doubt?

One of the beautiful virgins living in the empire was an orphan of exiled Jews, raised by her cousin Mordecai. Life's experiences had no doubt bruised her, but being taken as a part of the king's harem had to have been her greatest blow.

The book of Esther is silent about the person of God, but it is obvious that He is involved in the lives of the characters. What a statement this book makes about the reality of One Who continues to fulfill His perfect purpose in the lives of His people. Mervin Breneman wrote, "When we are most tempted to think that God has forgotten us . . . we can be sure that he is at work. . . . The point is that even before our problems arise, God has made provision for them."[3]

5. What in your life may have prompted you at some time to wonder why you are where you are, not living in another place, part of a different family?

How do you recognize God's hand in your life? Do you see that He has sovereignly directed your paths and that He asks you to serve Him in this place?

The Larger Story

What about Esther? Why were she and so many other Jews (perhaps as many as 15 million[4]) in Persia rather than in Jerusalem? Because of idolatry and sin, God allowed them to be captured by Nebuchadnezzar of Babylon.

6. What well-known Jewish boy was captured and taken from Israel to Babylon but refused to compromise himself before Nebuchadnezzar (Daniel 1:1–8)?

Seventy years after Nebuchadnezzar's victory over Jerusalem, Babylon was overcome by the Medo-Persians. At that time victorious Cyrus made a decree that allowed the Jews to return to their homeland, but comparatively few Jews took advantage of the opportunity.

The account of those who returned to the area of Jerusalem is recorded in the books of Ezra and Nehemiah. Zerubbabel and Joshua led the first return of Jewish people to Jerusalem about fifty years before the time of Esther. During this time, the prophets Haggai and Zechariah were preaching. Ezra and Nehemiah each led Jews back to Jerusalem shortly after the events of the book of Esther.

The promise of Jeremiah 29:11, "For I know the thoughts that I think toward you, says the LORD, thoughts of peace and not of evil, to give you a future and a hope," was written to the Jewish people while they were in captivity. What a wonderful promise is found in this verse and the verses surrounding it as God promises to gather the Jewish people again!

7. Why might so many Jews have chosen to stay in the land of their

captivity rather than returning to their homeland when return was offered?

The account recorded in the book of Esther involves the majority of Jews who chose to remain in Persia even after they were released from captivity and encouraged to return to Jerusalem. Perhaps they had achieved a place of physical and financial comfort. Perhaps the prospect of leaving the familiarity of a pagan land was more overwhelming than the freedom of returning to their homeland of Jerusalem.

Protected ID

8. Read Esther 2:9–11.
   (a) What favors did this young woman receive from the king's custodian of women (v. 9)?

   (b) What secret did this young woman keep, and why did she keep this secret (v. 10)?

   (c) Who was in place in Shushan to be concerned for Esther's welfare (v. 11)?

Unlike Daniel, also a Jew who lived in captivity decades earlier, Esther hid her Jewishness for the first five years she was in the palace. We are not told why Mordecai instructed her this way. By not revealing her identity, we must assume that she did not avoid the nonkosher foods of the palace and that she did not actively worship the God of Israel. We may assume that Esther had a nominal religious background but not enough to cause it to be a significant part of her life. She was a Jewish patriot and nationalist. Her "Jewishness was more a fact of birth than of religious conviction."[5]

To contemporary Jews, nationality and religion may be deemed worth dying for, but that sense of solidarity does not constitute a personal relationship with God. Esther was an entire generation removed from the exile to Babylon. I assume that she had not been taught the orthodox tenets of the law of Moses about living in relationship with Jehovah God. Since Mordecai had chosen to stay in Babylon rather than accept the opportunity that Cyrus, before Ahasuerus, offered to Jews to return to Jerusalem, we can guess that he may have chosen the comforts of life rather than a commitment to serve God wholeheartedly.

> There are, after all, in Israel today many "Mordecais" and "Esthers" who demonstrate great courage and nobility in their determination to die, if necessary, for the perpetuation of their nation and even of their religion. But it must also be sadly recognized that very few of these courageous Israelis know the God of their fathers in the sense of trusting in His provision of eternal salvation through the merits of the Messiah.[6]

Esther was a woman of extraordinary beauty and was used greatly by God. What encouragement there is in knowing that God chooses and uses people who do not even recognize that they are part of His plan. This is yet another facet of His hand at work.

Make It Personal

9. As you reflect upon your life and upon the time when you feared that God had forgotten you (question 4), how can you now see His protection even though you did not recognize that time as part of His plan? Write a brief prayer thanking God for His care and faithfulness during that time.

A Hidden Hand at Work

Remember, it was God Who raised a Jewish girl from obscurity to become queen of the most powerful empire in the world. Some of what we know about Esther and Mordecai can help us to suppose one reason God's name is not mentioned in this book. Perhaps the Jewish people at this time did not know Him well enough to draw His name into their daily lives.

In the days of Moses, God warned that He would hide His face from His people because of their disobedience (Deuteronomy 31:18). God's face is hidden in the book of Esther. Though the Jews of this book did not choose to return to Jerusalem, they were not beyond His care; He never abandoned them. Instead, He worked through them to preserve His people and fulfill His promise to provide a Deliverer. How thankful we should be that God's covenant reached His people even when they had been inconsistent and careless.

Take time regularly to thank God for dealing with you according to His promises rather than your performance. Even when you neglect prayer, Scripture, and commitment to Him, He never breaks His Word to you. He truly is the hero of this story. His faithful providence and presence are part of your life today.

Make It Personal

10. It is likely that God might be preparing you now for a future task. What can you begin doing right now to be better prepared for whatever He has for you?

11. What truths about God do you find in Jeremiah 29:11 and 14 that have implications for your life?

Notes

1. F. B. Huey, Jr., "Esther," edited by Frank E. Gaebelein, *The Expositor's Bible Commentary, Volume 4* (Grand Rapids: Zondervan, 1988), 804.

2. Joyce Baldwin, "Esther," edited by Donald Guthrie and Alex Motyer, *The New Bible Commentary: Revised* (Grand Rapids: Eerdmans, 1970), 415.

3. Breneman, 295.

4. Warren Wiersbe, *Be Committed* (Colorado Springs: Victor Books, 1993), 107.

5. Carey A. Moore, *Esther, The Anchor Bible Commentary* (Garden City, NY: Doubleday, 1971), LIV.

6. Whitcomb, 23.

LESSON

4

Only God . . . Chooses a Star

ESTHER 2:12–23

"For exaltation comes neither from the east nor from the west nor from the south. But God is the Judge: He puts down one, and exalts another" (Psalm 75:6, 7).

WITHOUT knowing the full story of someone's life, we are tempted to envy a person who has more luxuries, more privileges, and more opportunities than we do. Only after that person's life seems to crumble do we become aware of the heartaches, pressures, and manipulations that caused emptiness and depression. Though attractive, stardom is costly. Being chosen as a candidate for queen may sound like an enviable honor, but the cost to each of the contestants in Persia was great. That "honor" left them impoverished and indigent.

Esther, whose Persian name means "star," was about twenty-six years old when she went to the palace.[1] She was one of about four hundred women who began preparations for her night with the king.

The Competition

1. Read Esther 2:12–15.

(a) How long were Esther and the other young women given to prepare to meet with the king (v. 12)?

(b) What resources were available to all the young women (vv. 12, 13)?

(c) How did each young woman's location and status change after her time with King Ahasuerus (v. 14)?

(d) What determined whether a young woman would see the king again (v. 14)?

2. What do you learn about Esther from chapter 2, verses 7, 9, 10, 15, 17, and 20?

As the time approached for Esther's turn with the king, all emphasis was on physical beauty. Unlimited choices of jewelry, clothing, perfumes, and cosmetics were at her disposal. God's providential care was shown to Esther as He superintended preferential treatment of her. Hegai regarded her favorably, causing him to give her choice maids and to put her in the best place in the palace. Even at a time that must have seemed hopeless to Esther, God was at work, making this difficult time as smooth as it could be.

3. What did Esther choose to use as ornamentation when she went to the king (2:15)?

It was Esther's natural qualities of character and physical beauty, under God's providence, that caused her to be attractive to all who saw her.

A New Queen

4. Read Esther 2:16–18. What was the king's response to Esther, and what did he do?

Esther, a Jewess, became the Queen of Persia. Who, besides God, could have orchestrated such a chain of events? We continue to see Him in constant action. As a beautiful picture of His faithfulness, God repeatedly demonstrated His providence, His ultimate control, His ways that are higher than our ways.

Make It Personal

5. Recount a time in your life when God proved to you that He was at work in your life as "only God" could work.

Evil Exposed

During the king's great wedding feast in celebration of his new queen (v. 18), Mordecai was an official at the palace gate, the court for commercial and legal business.

While the king and his advisors were occupied with banqueting and celebrating, some disgruntled members of the palace staff plotted treachery.

6. Read Esther 2:19–23.

(a) What was the evil that Mordecai learned of (v. 21)?

(b) What did he do with that information (v. 22)?

(c) How would Mordecai have communicated such information to
    Queen Esther? (See chapter 2, verse 11.)

(d) What did Esther do with the information that came to her from
    Mordecai (v. 22)?

(e) What happened to the information that the palace received from
    Mordecai through Esther (v. 23)?

(f) Suppose that Mordecai had not been able to communicate to
    the palace about the plot he had discovered. What might have
    happened to the king, and what would have been the threat, then,
    for Esther?

Although Mordecai did not receive prompt recognition or reward for
his favor to the king, the palace scribe included Mordecai's discovery as
part of the official records of Persia. Picture the scene being set for the
king to owe a personal favor. See the hand of God at work. Who but God
would guarantee a permanent record of Mordecai's loyal deed? We will
learn later that it was God's providence that saved Mordecai's reward for
another time.

God's Orchestration of Events

In lesson 1 you recorded some circumstances in which you could see

God's hand at work as you read through Esther 1—10. In each of those circumstances, God's hand can be seen in directing or restraining events and people.

7. As a review, explain the significance of each of the following "happenings" of Esther 1 and 2 and tell the effect that each had upon the story as a whole.

(a) King Ahasuerus called for Vashti to display her beauty.

(b) Queen Vashti refused to obey the king's summons.

(c) The king and his advisors overreacted and deposed Vashti.

(d) A kingdom-wide search was made for a new queen.

(e) Esther, the Jewess, was so physically attractive.

(f) Hegai, the servant responsible for the king's harem, was partial toward Esther.

(g) The king chose Esther as his queen.

(h) Mordecai learned of the plot against the king.

(i) Mordecai's deed was recorded.

(j) Mordecai's reward was overlooked.

Only God can orchestrate the details of our lives so that all things work together for good. Only God can see the end from the beginning and put the pieces together in ways that "[accomplish] His purposes, but without in any way overriding the 'free' decisions and actions of the people involved."[2]

Make It Personal

8. Is there a seemingly unchangeable circumstance in your life—or the life of a loved one? If not, thank God for this time of peace and fullness as you are experiencing it now.

9. If there is a difficult, unresolved issue in your life, talk to the Lord about it and submit yourself to His will in this issue. Invite Him to grant you patience and long-suffering to accomplish His will in you as you wait upon Him and seek His leading and enabling in the circumstance.

Notes
1. Whitcomb, 49.

2. Baldwin, 414.

5

Devising Destruction

ESTHER 3

"The Lord shall preserve you from all evil; He shall preserve your soul. The Lord shall preserve your going out and your coming in from this time forth, and even forevermore"
(Psalm 121:7, 8).

IN THE early years of my husband's first pastorate, a woman in our church became very angry about a decision that he made. Although the decision did not pertain to her in any personal or targeted way, she allowed her anger to dictate her reaction. She threatened to destroy his reputation as punishment for his unwillingness to change his decision. Blessed by God's protection, her threats never reached a willing or powerful audience.

It is a dangerous thing to become so angry and so hurt that you want to make others pay for the wrong you think has been done against you. It is especially dangerous when this obsession with revenge belongs to someone who actually has the position and resources to manipulate a situation so that others are powerless to defend themselves.

At the beginning of chapter 3, four years after Esther was crowned queen, a new man was promoted as the king's chief officer of the Persian Empire. With the promotion, King Ahasuerus gave great authority to this man.

1. Compare Esther 1:13 and 14 with 3:1. What change in names do you find in chapter 3?

It is ironic that it is Haman who received the honor of promotion. At the end of chapter 2, a reader might reasonably expect Mordecai to be the one who would receive honor and recognition. Consider the hand of God at work even in this situation as He allowed Haman to be elevated to this high position.

An Elevated Man

2. Read Esther 3:1–15. What do you learn about Haman? Note as many details as you can.

-

-

-

-

-

3. Read Proverbs 6:16–19. What seven things that God hates are named in these verses?

-

-

-

-

-

-

-

4. What behaviors or attitudes from your Proverbs 6 list appear in Haman's words and deeds in Esther chapter 3? Next to each characteristic you identified from Proverbs 6 (question 3), note the verse references from Esther 3 where you see an example from Haman's life.

Antagonisms

5. According to Esther 2:5 and 3:1, what identities are given to Mordecai and to Haman?

From the use of the words "a certain Jew" and "the Agagite," a current as well as foreshadowed tension between the men seems to be implied. Haman, the villain in the story, was an Agagite, a descendant of Agag, king of the Amalekites (1 Samuel 15:8). According to Exodus 17, the Amalekites attacked the Children of Israel at Rephidim after God

delivered His Chosen People from enslavement in Egypt (v. 8). While
Aaron and Hur supported Moses' hands, Moses interceded for Israel and
Joshua led the army in battle against the Amalekite attackers. God gave
victory to the Israelites.

Moses quoted God as saying, "I will utterly blot out the remembrance
of Amalek from under heaven" and that He would have "war with Amalek
from generation to generation" (Exodus 17:14, 16). In 1 Samuel 15 God
commanded Saul, the first king of Israel, to destroy the Amalekites, but
because of Saul's disobedience, some of them lived.

6. What does Esther 3:2 say that King Ahasuerus commanded his
servants to do?

It seems odd that a customary expression of respect for office would
need to be dictated. It is suspected that there was "a general lack of respect" for Haman.[1] His pride and vanity apparently prompted him to seek
and demand recognition and honor beyond what he had earned. As the
story unfolds, it seems that Haman is most concerned with his own power
and importance.

Resistance

7. According to Esther 3:3 and 4, who refused to obey the dictate of
the king?

When questioned by other servants, Mordecai revealed his ancestry.
Why? What explanation for his behavior toward Haman could that offer?
As a Jew was he forbidden to bow?

Remember who Haman was—an Amalekite. This was not merely

a personal grudge or a battle of individuals. Mordecai's resistance to Haman's expectations was likely an expression of an ancestral feud, a conflict between Jews and Amalekites, between good and evil, between the purposes of God and the purposes of Satan. The Jews were God's Chosen People; Satan made them his target and wanted them destroyed.

Mordecai, a descendant of Saul (compare Esther 2:5 and 1 Samuel 9:1, 2), made a strong statement when he announced his Jewish blood. Because of his probable lifestyle (as discussed in lesson 3), we may assume that Mordecai's stand was due to his nationalism rather than to personal allegiance to Jehovah. Customarily, Jewish people were submissive in bowing to those in authority, not as an act of worship but of civil obedience. In this case, Haman's ancestry was as much a factor as Mordecai's. Haman was not only an enemy of Mordecai but of all Jews.

A Schemer's Scheme

8. What was Haman's response to Mordecai's refusal to pay him honor (3:5, 6)?

According to verses 3 and 4, Mordecai received daily pressure to give homage to Haman, but he stood his ground firmly and courageously in the conflict. His refusal to submit to the king's command probably stemmed from "his refusal to be subservient, as a Jew, to the ancient enemy."[2]

Make It Personal

9. Have you ever felt about anyone as Haman did about Mordecai? If so, how did you handle that relationship?

The visible conflict shows Haman, an enemy of the Jews, fighting against Mordecai and the Jewish people. Just as active but less visible, another conflict unfolds with Satan and his demonic host fighting against God and the heavenly host.

Behind this conflict between Haman and Mordecai, between the evil element in Persia and the nation of Israel, was a battle that has continued since the Garden of Eden. Satan, God's adversary, is ever the aggressor; and in this conflict he is promoting his prize fighter, Haman.[3]

Make It Personal

10. How does the world system pressure you to compromise in living a God-pleasing life today? What do you have to risk or give up in order to remain true to the things you value most?

11. How can you better prepare yourself to stand up for your beliefs in spite of pressure or persecution?

A Scheme

12. Not satisfied to condemn Mordecai alone, Haman nurtured his hate and vengeful prejudice until he formulated a plan that would be far more extensive. What did he want to accomplish through it (3:6)?

13. As Haman devised a plot to destroy the entire Jewish population, how did he determine the timing? According to verse 7, what did he do to decide the date of destruction?

Casting of lots was part of Persian custom. Haman would have believed that the success of an important plan depended on cooperation with a "lucky day." Pur, cube-shaped dice, were used to choose dates for significant events.

An Unseen Hand

Although Haman cast lots and supposedly received direction from the Persian gods, astrologers, and magicians, God's hand was in control even of the lots, as the date chosen was yet eleven months away.

14. What reassurance could God's people have because of Proverbs 16:33?

15. Haman used a mixture of truth, innuendo, error, and exaggeration in his scheme to convince the king of an impending threat. When presenting his plot to Ahasuerus, how did Haman misrepresent the Jews (Esther 3:8)?

Did Haman make it sound like these people were dangerous, rebellious, and guilty of breaking all the laws of the land? This was quite a case of exaggeration. He did not even name the people group, but was quite vague in his description and made the situation sound urgent.

A King's Misplaced Confidence

Ahasuerus characteristically relied too heavily on others and made impetuous decisions that he regretted later. His response to Haman's recommendation was no exception. How could a ruler be so careless? He acted like a puppet on a string, allowing himself to be manipulated by the semblance of power. He did not even ask questions. He did not inquire as to which laws had been broken. He did not ask about which people group was about to be destroyed.

With little trouble, Haman bought the future of the Jews. Without thought, Ahasuerus complied with a deadly scheme. Haman offered a great amount of money to the empire's treasury from the plunder of the Jews' possessions and confiscated property.

16. How is Haman described in verse 10?

Bad News Broadcasted

No time was wasted. The king gave Haman his signet ring and full authority to write the decree. When a king's seal was used, it was the equivalent of a signature. The decree for the destruction of the Jews was written, sealed, and delivered to the 127 provinces of Persia (vv. 12–15).

17. What were the details of the decree composed by Haman (v. 13)?

18. How was this order made known across the realm (v. 15)?

19. What effect did this order have on the city of Shushan, the king's citadel (v. 15)?

What a contrast can be seen in this drama as chapter 3 ends. "On the one hand the nonchalant king and courtier with their wine; on the other the people of the city, apprehensive at the publication of so arbitrary an edict."[4]

Make It Personal

20. Read Romans 8:28.
(a) Thank God for allowing you to see many ways He worked in the book of Esther to this point. Thank Him for His continued sovereignty in your life as well.

(b) What have you learned about the Lord from your study of the
    book of Esther so far?

Notes

1. Joyce Baldwin, *Esther: An Introduction and Commentary* (Downers
Grove, IL: InterVarsity Press, 1984), 72.

2. McConville, 166.

3. Larry Green, *In Sovereign Hands,* Adult Teacher (Schaumburg, IL: Regular
Baptist Press, 1992), 65.

4. Baldwin, *The New Bible Commentary Revised,* 417.

LESSON

6

Choosing Commitment with Courage

ESTHER 4

"And Mordecai told them to answer Esther: Do not think in your heart that you will escape in the king's palace any more than all the other Jews. For if you remain completely silent at this time, relief and deliverance will arise for the Jews from another place, but you and your father's house will perish. Yet who knows whether you have come to the kingdom for such a time as this?" (Esther 4:13, 14).

ABORTIONS, starvations, tsunami victims, hurricane refugees. There are so many urgent needs, so many crises. How can an individual know where to get involved? How can one person make a difference in a situation involving thousands and even millions of other people? God sovereignly puts us in places where we can obey Him and make a difference for what is right.

The horrific news of the decree that all Jews—including young and old, women and children—should be killed, plundered, and annihilated (3:13) spread quickly through the empire of Persia. All people from India to Ethiopia were notified of the decree. There may have been as many as 15 million Jews living under Persian rule.[1] Can you imagine receiving this news of impending doom for yourself, your entire family, and your nation?

Mordecai had already revealed his Jewish identity to the king's servants.

69

Now he needed a plan of action that would identify him with the death sentence upon all Jews, allow him an audience with the queen, and make his position clear.

Impact of the Decree

1. Read Esther 4:1–3. How did the Jews throughout the empire demonstrate their hopelessness (v. 3)?

2. How did Mordecai, living in the capital city, express the impact of the decree upon him (v. 1, 2)?

Mordecai marched through the city to the king's gate in protest of the decree. Because of his clothing, he was not permitted to enter the gate. As queen, Esther was secluded from outside happenings, so it was necessary for Mordecai to try to attract attention from other people living within the palace. Esther's maids and servants witnessed his actions and notified the queen. Although neither Esther nor her servants knew Mordecai's reasons for mourning clothes and wailing, she sent different clothing to him. Mordecai did not accept Esther's offer. That refusal aroused greater attention and eventually allowed him the privilege of a conversation with Esther through her messenger.

Urgent Exchanges

3. Read Esther 4:4–9. Who was entrusted with the conversation between the queen and her cousin (vv. 5, 6)?

4. Realizing that Esther and Mordecai were not able to speak to each other directly, what might be assumed about the character of the messenger?

Mordecai knew the facts of the decree. He knew about Haman's promise of money for the king's treasury from the anticipated plunder of the Jews. And he had a copy of the decree for Esther to read. Can you see the hand of God again? Mordecai's position within the palace ("within the king's gate," 3:2) had allowed him to be very familiar with legal affairs and to have accurate information to pass into Esther's hands.

5. Mordecai's instructions to Esther were forceful. What message did he send to her through Hathach (vv. 7–9)?

Situation Critical

6. Read Esther 4:10–14. Mordecai was convinced that Esther should appeal to the king personally. Her response was a reminder to Mordecai of her precarious position. What caused Esther to be hesitant to approach the king (vv. 10, 11)?

Even though Esther was the queen chosen by Ahasuerus, she did not have access to the king unless he initiated it. Persian law dictated that unsummoned intruders were liable to death. Her husband was unpredictable and had not even called for his queen during the past month.

> Isolated as she was in the harem, she had few ways of knowing what political concerns were occupying him, what mood he was in, or whether another of his women was his current favorite.[2]

Esther risked being accused—just as Vashti had been—of disobedience, of being a bad example, of rebellion and disrespect to the nation's
laws. "Was she not committing in this act a similar crime as Vashti, the
previous queen? Vashti had not come when called; Esther was coming
when not called!"[3]

As Mordecai urged Esther to approach the king, we see a strengthening of his perspective. Had he simply grown wiser, or did he finally recognize the hand of God in the unfolding of events? Did he recall teachings
of God's promises to Israel and become convinced that the promises to
Abraham, Moses, and David would not be fulfilled if the nation were oblit-
erated? Did he recognize God and His providence?

Mordecai was a committed patriot on behalf of his Jewish nation.
Though not righteous in his dealings before God, he apparently had a
sense of the covenant relationship between God and the Jewish people. As
we read Esther 4, we can almost watch the strengthening of Mordecai's
respect for and confidence in God's purposes and program.

7. What do verses 13 and 14 disclose about Mordecai?

His challenge to Esther can be seen as a turning of allegiance. Mordecai finally seemed to remember what was important. His great sense of
need turned his thoughts, attention, and loyalty back to the "relief and deliverance" of the God of his fathers (v. 14). In three sentences, Mordecai
appealed to Esther with three weighty truths. Remember, Esther had been
reared by Mordecai; he knew her well and was confident of her character
as he expressed truths about the perilous situation.

8. According to verse 14, what three things did Mordecai want Esther
to consider?
   (a) What would happen to her personally if she did not act on behalf
       of her people?

(b) What would happen to the Jews if she did not get involved?

(c) How could she help?

The Hand of Providence

If Mordecai experienced a spiritual awakening, he tried to transfer that to Esther. He tried to help her see that she was not in the palace by accident but that there had been a hand of Providence arranging people and events during the five years she had been the queen of Ahasuerus. All that Mordecai had heard and known became clear as he began to understand that Someone must have included all of these remarkable events within His sovereign and unfailing plan. Mordecai had only a few minutes and a messenger in order to convey his realization to Esther.

9. Mordecai realized that there was a clear and high purpose for Esther's presence in the palace. Why was she really there (v. 14)?

10. Mordecai recognized a surety in the providence of God and in God's providential timing. What was his question to Esther in verse 14, and what would this question communicate to Esther?

Mordecai's words to Esther should remind us that nothing happens in our lives before it has passed through the hand of God. As Dr. R. T. Ketcham loved to quote, God is "too wise to make a mistake, and too loving to be unkind." He uses and chooses people and situations to fulfill His purposes in this world and even makes evil cooperate in producing good.

Warren Wiersbe has noted "some basic truths about the providence of God that are important for Christians today.

• God has divine purposes to accomplish.

• God accomplishes His purposes through people.

• God will accomplish His purposes even if His servants refuse to obey His will.

• God isn't in a hurry but will fulfill His plans in due time."[4]

Decision, Please

11. Read Esther 4:15–17. How did Esther communicate her decision to Mordecai (v. 15)?

It was time for Esther to send her answer to Mordecai. She had to decide if she were willing to risk her life in hopes of saving the Jewish people.

> This must, therefore, be recognized as Esther's moment of destiny. Mordecai's plea was irresistible. The promises of God, the justice of God, and the providence of God shine brilliantly through the entire crisis, so that the mere omission of His name obscures nothing of His identity, attributes, and purposes for His chosen people and for the entire world of mankind.[5]

Esther had received the import of Mordecai's message and understood that she was equally at risk whether she remained silent or approached the king. She also seemed to realize the weight of a spiritual conflict. Her words in verse 16 are not fatalistic; they communicate her "determination which sees that faith permits only one course of action."[6]

12. What two things did Esther ask Mordecai to do (v. 16)?

Esther's request for her people to show their support of her mission by fasting (v. 16) implies that she was also asking others to pray. Her request shows that she relied on the support of others and did not assume that she could accomplish this great task alone. Esther is to be admired greatly for her submission and courage at such a defining moment.

Make It Personal

13. Reflect on a time when you struggled to do what was right. In what area of your life do you currently need to do what is right and trust God with the outcome?

14. Sometimes we seem to be at the mercy of another person, such as a policeman, judge, other government official, teacher, boss, or husband. Whether you are in a courtroom or asking for a raise or requesting permission for something, how can you trust God to work in the heart of the individual who seems to control the decision?

15. What assurance of God's sovereignty and authority is expressed in Proverbs 21:1?

The last few verses of Esther 4 are pivotal and represent the central message of the story: God's people would be delivered. God had promised to preserve and protect them, and His providence would not allow that promise to fail.[7]

Even though the situation looked impossible, God had prepared the people He had chosen, and He used them to accomplish His purpose. When Esther realized this, she reached the point of commitment. When faced with a difficult decision, she nobly and courageously chose to obey.

16. What did Esther commit herself to do (v. 16)?

Make It Personal

"Lord, please use me for Your honor and glory. Prepare me through trials of life so I will be ready. Take me in death whenever it pleases You. Carry out Your plan through my life."

Can you pray this for yourself? Can you pray it for your children and grandchildren? May we desire lives that are totally yielded to the purposes of God.

Notes

1. Wiersbe, 107.

2. *Ruth & Esther,* Life Change Series (Colorado Springs: NavPress, 1987), 98. Used by permission of NavPress—www.navpress.com. All rights reserved.

3. Gary Cohen, "Esther: The Book," *Zion's Fire,* March–April, 1997, 17.

4. Wiersbe, 112, 113.

5. Whitcomb, 78, 79.

6. McConville, 172.

7. Larry Green, *In Sovereign Hands,* Adult Student (Schaumburg, IL: Regular Baptist Press, 1992), 98.

LESSON

7

Too Late
to Turn Back

ESTHER 5

"The king's heart is in the hand of the LORD, like the rivers of water; He turns it wherever He wishes" (Proverbs 21:1).

AFTER agreeing to participate in worthy causes, I have been tempted sometimes to reconsider and look for someone to take my place. Being part of the leadership seemed noble and directed by God at the time I made the commitment, but now . . . as the time gets closer, I find myself asking, "What was I thinking?"

As soon as Esther decided her course and committed herself to be involved in trying to save the lives of her people the Jews, she invested her next forty hours in preparation to approach King Ahasuerus. She, her maids, Mordecai, and the Jews of their city fasted over a span of three days. Although prayer is not mentioned, it is presumed that many Jews prayed as they fasted.

> Jews in the Old Testament often resorted to fasting in periods of stress. . . . Since prayer frequently accompanied fasting, Esther was certainly asking, in effect, for the Jewish community to intercede with God on her behalf.[1]

The Queen's Great Risk

1. Read Esther 5:1–8. As King Ahasuerus saw Esther, her courage was rewarded.

(a) What did the king do (vv. 2, 3)?

(b) What was Esther's response (vv. 4, 5)?

2. Read Proverbs 21:1. How is this verse illustrated at this point in the account of Esther?

At the moment Esther defied Persian law and approached her husband uninvited, she put her life at risk. The threat of death and the hope of life were equally present. She summoned great courage and seized the initiative by entering the palace court and waiting for the king's reception. The king's extension of his golden scepter was the only response that could spare her life. Even though Esther appeared to approach the king alone, God accompanied her, providentially protecting her and preparing the way for her intercession.

Esther responded to the king's acceptance of her uninvited presence; she touched the tip of the scepter as an expression of gratitude and respect. The scepter was the only means of Esther's physical salvation. What a beautiful picture of God's grace to us!

Compare the offer of the scepter by the king with the grace of God toward us. God's grace is offered to a lost world through the blood of Jesus Christ. Without that blood we cannot enter God's presence; but because of it, our lives are touched and we are given the great gift of access to Him.

Make It Personal

3. As we think of God's grace extended to us, we must not forget to appreciate and respect Him. List two or three ways your life has been touched by the scepter of God's grace.

-

-

-

Have you responded by accepting His gift of grace?

The Next Steps

Undoubtedly, the king was surprised to see Esther. Thinking that she had an urgent need that prompted her to take such an unusual risk, Ahaseurus prompted her to voice her petition. He even promised her in advance that her request would be granted.

Only part of her mission was accomplished. Esther had received an audience with the king, but the responsibility of her forthcoming petition was weighty. In the process of interceding for her people, Esther still needed to:

- "make a request for the change of a law, which, according to Persian custom, could not be done;
- reveal herself as a Jew;
- place herself in opposition to . . . Haman," [2] an all-powerful favorite of the king.

4. Instead of verbalizing these things at the banquet she had initiated, what did Esther request (vv. 6–8)?

The seriousness of the rest of Esther's mission demanded discretion and careful planning. She had prepared a private banquet to which she invited the king and Haman. She was familiar with the king's priorities and his decision-making practices and knew it was crucial that she announce her request in a private setting.

5. Does Esther's action seem odd? How is her response in verses 7 and 8 different from what you might have expected?

Esther's actions are not consistent with a reader's expectations. A first-time reader of this history would probably anticipate that Esther would seize the earliest moment and make her request while her presence was welcome. Her surprising plan is effective in heightening interest and curiosity as well as portraying her patience, wisdom, and awareness.

God's Hand Continues at Work

During the successful banquet with the king and Haman, his right-hand man, Esther seemed to change her mind; she suddenly postponed her petition and invited both men to another banquet the following day. That postponement was evidence of God's directing Esther. His hand was at work in causing her to wait.

Can you see God's hand continuing to ready the stage for the queen's successful intercession? The king has agreed to return the second day. No one has told Haman of Esther's heritage. Haman's conceit has increased to the point of recklessness. The plot thickens, but God's hand is still obvious. Esther demonstrated increased courage as she prepared for the opportunity of greatest influence.

Make It Personal

6. Where has God has placed you?

(a) Is there an area in which you need to demonstrate courage?

(b) Do you need to be patient and wait for God's timing?

(c) What risks are involved?

Haman in His Glory

Haman left the queen's first banquet, strutting like a proud peacock. It was a wonderful day for him and everything seemed to be going his way. He was at the height of his career, filled with pride and happiness.

7. Read Esther 5:9–14.

(a) What was Haman proud of (vv. 9–11)?

(b) How did he display that pride (vv. 10–12)?

Haman is a prime example of the world's happiness. Without an awareness of God's grace, the world's happiness is dependent upon circumstances. It is shallow and temporary, causing extreme shifts in moods and personality. How easily it is altered.

8. Within minutes, what ruined Haman's happiness as he left the palace and headed home (v. 13)?

In conversation with his wife and friends, Haman bragged about his riches, his family, his power, and his prominence. While reciting his wealth, he also complained about Mordecai. "Haman's preoccupation with revenge blocked out for him all his other blessings." [3]

Someone has said that the size of a man's character is determined by the size of the things that irritate him. Haman was at the height of his career as the second most prominent man in the empire. Why was he so preoccupied with Mordecai's refusal to stand and acknowledge him? Haman was a man filled with prejudice. To Haman, Mordecai represented the entire Jewish race, and Haman was consumed by his hatred of Jews.

Make It Personal

9. If there something in your life that dulls the edge of your joy and keeps you from enjoying all that you have in Christ, what is it?

Haman's wife and friends encouraged him to stop whining, to use his position and power, and to do something. If he could arrange the elimination of an entire race, he certainly could find a way to remedy his present aggravation with one man.

Hangman's Shadow

10. What did Haman's wife and friends suggest (v. 14)?

Haman put their suggestion into motion. Workers began the construction of gallows seventy-five feet high for the purpose of hanging Mordecai as an example and warning to the rest of the Jews. Haman's hatred had prompted him to devise another exaggerated scheme.

To a first-time reader, all hope must seem lost. Esther has not yet told the king about her relationship to Mordecai and the other Jews. The king does not remember that Mordecai had saved his life. Haman plans to have Mordecai executed the next morning. Though the situation looks hopeless, what we must remember as we read is that God is there, still working, still using His hand to accomplish His purpose.

Notes

1. Moore, 51.

2. James Martin Gray, *Christian Workers' Commentary on the Whole Bible* (Westwood, NJ: Fleming H. Revell Co., 1953), 209.

3. Moore, 60, 61.

LESSON

8

From Sleeplessness to Celebration

ESTHER 6

"Therefore humble yourselves under the mighty hand of God, that He may exalt you in due time, casting all your care upon Him, for He cares for you" (1 Peter 5:6, 7).

SLEEPLESSNESS. Did you have too much caffeine? Are you carrying anxiety and burdens? Are you fearful and uneasy? Does God want you to pray? Does He remind you of something? Does He prompt new ideas and dreams? Though I am tempted to view periods of sleeplessness as unproductive and as a waste of precious time designated for rest, God repeatedly brings good from those quiet hours.

1. Read Esther 6:1–3. What was the king's situation (v. 1)?

Perhaps King Ahasuerus was not able to sleep because he wondered about Esther's request. Perhaps he could not sleep because of the noise from the building of the gallows. Whatever the human distraction, God caused the king to have insomnia during the night between Esther's two banquets.

84

A Matter of Honor

2. What was ordered as a hopeful antidote for the king's sleeplessness (v. 1)?

God's providence can be seen clearly. He prevented the king from sleeping, and He used that insomnia to accomplish the turning point of the book of Esther. Most of the main characters are not even present for this pivotal moment. Without doubt, God alone is in control.

3. As a result of being unable to sleep, what did the king discover (v. 2)?

The Persians kept careful records of all events pertaining to the palace and the empire. This event had happened and had been recorded more than four years earlier (2:21–23). Can you see the hand of God at work in bringing Mordecai's particular deed to the king's attention that particular night? Can you see the hand of God in even preventing a reward at the time of the deed? It was considered to be an honorable thing for the king to reward good deeds, so Ahasuerus' oversight toward Mordecai reflected poorly on himself, and he wanted to rectify that immediately. Only the providence of God could have saved the reward for this hour.

Make It Personal

4. What kinds of things have contributed to times of sleeplessness in your life? Why might God have permitted you to go through any of those times of sleeplessness?

The morning came, and Haman arrived at the palace early. "This is arguably the most ironically comic scene in the entire Bible,"[1] observed Karen Jobes. Neither the king nor Haman was aware of the other man's motives and plans for Mordecai. Only the readers are fully aware of the conflicting purposes and intentions.

A Counselor and His Counsel

5. Read Esther 6:4–9.

(a) Why did Haman arrive so early, and what did he come to suggest (v. 4)?

(b) What did the king ask Haman (v. 6), and whom did he have in mind (v. 3)?

(c) What did Haman suggest in response to the king's request for counsel (vv. 7–9)?

(d) Whom did Haman have in mind to receive such honor (v. 6)?

Haman entered the king's chamber ready to make his request, but the king spoke first. We may assume that the king would have consulted any advisor who had been present. The hand of God put Haman there as the one who was available.

What irony is obvious to the readers! While Haman was plotting a man's death, the king was planning that same man's reward, but their mutual preoccupations prevented them from understanding. As Haman's pride continued to inflate, he was asked to give personal advice about *what* should be rewarded, but he was oblivious as to the king's choice of *who* would receive the reward.

Haman's heart was fully controlled by his own pride that caused him to detail the way honor should be shown. Thinking only of himself as the intended recipient, Haman suggested an elaborate form of exaltation. He wanted to wear the king's robe while he rode the king's horse. He wanted to be served by a noble prince and displayed throughout the city.

Did Haman want it to appear as if he were the king? Perhaps he wanted the people of Shushan to see him as the king's choice of a successor. He was missing only a crown on his head, but he called for a crown on the head of the horse he would be riding.

Roles Reversed

6. Read Esther 6:10 and 11. What instructions did the king give to Haman (v. 10)?

7. What irony is evident in the instructions?

The king responded favorably to Haman's counsel, but he had a different recipient in mind. Instead of being honored, Haman was humiliated. Instead of being executed, Mordecai was exalted. Again, only God could orchestrate such a turn of events.

From Exalted to Abased

Irony follows irony. Not only had Haman decided how the man he desired to hang would be honored, but he was assigned as Mordecai's servant. What Mordecai had refused to do for Haman (bowing before him),

Haman had to command others to do for Mordecai. Haman's arrogance and conditional happiness changed to misery.

8. Read Esther 6:12–14. After Haman paraded Mordecai through the city and the men parted, where did each of them go (v. 12)?

In sharp contrast to the manner of his return from the queen's banquet the evening before, Haman was embarrassed and mournful when he returned from announcing Mordecai's honor throughout the city at the order of the king. His "friends" of the previous day became his "wise men" (5:10; 6:13). Their counsel to him was accurate and portrayed a specific portion of the prophecy of Genesis 12:2 and 3.

9. Read Genesis 12:2 and 3. What was that prophecy, and how did it apply to Mordecai?

Zeresh, Haman's wife, verbalized a central theme of the book of Esther when she predicted Haman's destruction as an enemy of the Jews. Even she acknowledged the assurance of God's protection of His people. Mordecai represents the Jews; Haman represents the enemy who cannot prevail against him but will surely fall before him (6:13).

Haman's pride and evil plotting against the Jewish people had not gone unnoticed by God. He was not unaware of Haman's pride, his evil manipulations, his prejudicial motives, his false security in himself, and his arrogant stand against the Jewish people. God's faithfulness to His people guaranteed their deliverance and Haman's failure.

10. Envision Haman as the time approached for Esther's second banquet (6:14; 7:1) and speculate on his state of mind.

The sequence of events makes it clear that King Ahasuerus was not aware of the tension between Mordecai and Haman. Although the king knew that Mordecai was a Jew, he was still ignorant of the fact that the decree he had signed was against the Jewish people.

The irony of such a day! Haman's dream of exaltation for himself was given to the one he hated most. Instead of being served by a "most noble prince," Haman became that servant. Haman's plan had been to have Mordecai executed so he could enjoy fully the queen's banquet. Instead, he spent the hours leading up to the banquet displaying the honor of Mordecai.

Even as Haman was summoned from his home to the palace, the gallows built speedily at his command stood unused but ready.

Make It Personal

11. God places much emphasis upon people knowing Him as He has revealed Himself (Jeremiah 9:23, 24; Hosea 6:6; John 17:3; 20:31). How can depending upon God as He has revealed Himself sustain you in life's trials? Consider the verses that follow.

(a) Psalm 32:8

(b) Jeremiah 33:3

(c) Nahum 1:7

(d) John 20:31

(e) Hebrews 4:15, 16

(f) 1 Peter 5:7

Notes
   1. Jobes, 152.

9

More Surprises as the Day Continues

ESTHER 7

"Do not be deceived, God is not mocked; for whatever a man sows, that he will also reap" (Galatians 6:7).

NOT EVERY day goes according to plan. Some days take quick turns and others just slowly decline. A day with my granddaughter flies by much too quickly, but day in a waiting room seems to last a week. Esther had come too far to change her mind. What would happen next? What more could one day hold?

The day of reckoning continued. Just one day before, Esther had adorned herself in her royal robes, had stood before the king uninvited, and had requested that he and Haman attend her banquet. It was only the preceding night that Haman had built the gallows and that King Ahasuerus had not slept and so had learned of the honor due to Mordecai.

It was only earlier that day that the lives of Haman and Mordecai began to be reversed. Just a few hours before, Haman had been forced to honor Mordecai the Jew by leading him throughout the city in kingly garments and riding the king's horse. In less than one day Haman had gone from honored official to humiliated servant. All of his reversal revolved around his pride and prejudice.

As the king and Haman attended Esther's second private banquet in as many days, King Ahasuerus asked Esther for the third time to state her request. And for the third time, he promised to be generous in granting it.

The Queen's Petition

1. Read Esther 7:1–4.

(a) What were the main points of Esther's petition (v. 3)?

(b) What was the extreme circumstance that prompted her to make this plea (v. 4)?

Esther was clothed in strength, humility, and dignity as she courageously presented her request. She focused her petition on the fact that her life was in danger. She identified herself with an entire race of people who were endangered, and she quoted accurately from the original decree. She made reference to the fact that Haman had offered the king a price in exchange for the privilege of destroying her and her people.

Again, the hand of God can be seen in the postponement of Esther's plea at the first banquet. It is now clearly seen that God delayed her petition until the king had been reminded of Mordecai's deed and had been given reason to honor a Jew. Such perfect timing!

The Plot Unravels

2. Read Esther 7:5–7. What words did Esther use to describe Haman (v. 6)?

Haman must have been surprised beyond description. When he had asked for the lives of the Jewish people, he did not have any idea that he was including the life of the queen. When the king asked Esther who was to blame for the plot, she pointedly indicted Haman.

3. The king's surprise and anger at this revelation caused him to retreat to the adjoining garden. Imagine and list some of the things that Ahasuerus might have realized in those moments.

•

•

•

Verdict and Sentence

4. Read Esther 7:7–10. While the king was in the palace garden, trying to come to terms with what Esther had revealed, what was Haman doing (v. 7)?

Haman immediately realized that his only hope was to convince the queen to intercede for him. How ironic that Esther and Haman would plead for their lives at the same banquet! Haman, who had hatred for the Jews and a devious scheme for their execution, not only had to lead a Jew through the streets in honor, but also had to plead for his life from one he had sentenced to death—all on the same day! Haman had been incensed because a Jewish man would not bow down before him. Now he was prostrate himself before a Jewish woman as he begged for his life. Readers have anticipated Esther's plea with hope and support, but Haman's plea comes as a surprise.

Sowing and Reaping

It was at that moment that King Ahasuerus returned to the room. He accused Haman of inappropriate behavior toward the queen and spoke the word that commanded his execution.

5. Read Esther 7:8–10. Haman was arrested immediately and sentenced to death for his conduct toward the queen. Was Haman guilty of the crime for which he was accused and punished (v. 8)?

The king exaggerated Haman's crime of assaulting the queen. This exaggeration is similar in proportion to Haman's misrepresentation of the crimes of the Jews in Esther 3:8.

One of the attendants at the banquet drew the king's attention to the gallows, which could be seen from the palace. Haman had apparently boasted of the purpose for which he had built the gallows. Immediately there were three strikes against Haman:

• Manipulation of the king for the decree against the Jews
• Inappropriate action toward the queen
• A plan to execute Mordecai

6. The king, who usually made decisions by relying on those around him, followed Harbonna's suggestion for Haman's death. What command did he issue (v. 9)?

What an ironic day! In the morning Haman had led Mordecai, dressed in the king's robe, through the streets on the king's horse. Before the day ended, Haman, with his face covered, was led through the same streets to the gallows he had constructed.

When this gallows was built, it was to give Haman an occasion for exulting in his perceived superiority (5:14). Instead, it became the instrument of his own death.

7. One of the great principles of Scripture is clearly illustrated in Haman's life. Read Galatians 6:7. What did Haman reap from his anger, vengeance, and desire to kill? Explain.

Psalm 9:15 and 16 praise God for victory over enemies: "In the net which they hid, their own foot is caught. The LORD is known by the judgment He executes; the wicked is snared in the work of his own hands." Haman was caught in his own net. His pride and prejudice dominated his life and ultimately destroyed him.

Make It Personal

8. Haman is no character to emulate. In fact, the Scriptures convey many warnings about where pride and anger lead. What warnings do you see for yourself in these verses?

(a) Proverbs 29:23

(b) Ecclesiastes 7:9

(c) Ephesians 4:26

(d) Philippians 2:3

Haman, the enemy, was dead, but Esther's request for her life and the life of her people had not been granted. The date of the Jews' annihilation was almost nine months away, but the decree stood unchanged and unchangeable.

Only God could bring the justice of chapter 7. Although the details of His solution are yet to unfold, readers have confidence that God is working and that He will assure that Esther's petition to the king is granted.

In lesson 5 you recorded circumstances in which the hand of God was apparent in chapters 1 and 2. Additional situations have unfolded in Esther chapters 3—7.

9. Why is each of the following details significant to the story?

(a) Haman was elevated to a place of great authority (3:1).

(b) The date for elimination of the Jewish race was still eleven months away when the original decree was published (3:8–15).

(c) Mordecai's position in the palace allowed him to have a personal copy of the decree (4:8).

(d) The king extended his scepter to Esther (5:1, 2).

(e) Esther did not voice her request at the first banquet (5:6–8).

(f) No one told Haman that Esther was a Jew.

(g) Haman's pride and conceit increased because of Esther's invitation (5:9–12).

(h) Haman passed Mordecai on his way home after he had perceived himself to be elevated yet again in the king's favor (5:9).

(i) Haman built gallows (5:14).

(j) King Ahasuerus had insomnia before Esther revealed her petition (6:1).

(k) Haman arrived at the palace early the next morning (6:1–3).

When God revealed to His prophet Jeremiah that the exile of his people would be limited to seventy years, He assured the Jews of His purposes toward them: "For I know the thoughts that I think toward you, says the LORD, thoughts of peace and not of evil, to give you a future and a hope" (Jeremiah 29:11). Even in the most difficult times of life, we must remember and trust what God has revealed about His character and His sovereign ways, His perfect plans and purposes. Weeping may endure for a night, but we wait in faith for Him to bring joy in the morning (Psalm 30:5).

10

Wait! What about the Decree?

ESTHER 8

"For I am persuaded that neither death nor life, nor angels nor principalities nor powers, nor things present nor things to come, nor height nor depth, nor any other created thing, shall be able to separate us from the love of God which is in Christ Jesus our Lord" (Romans 8:38, 39).

TAKE some pain pills and get some sleep. Yes, there is temporary relief, but you awaken with recurring pain. Go out for dinner with close friends and talk about good times, but a temporary celebration fades with the realization that a serious problem still exists.

We cheer and applaud Esther's victory over Haman, but wait! Has anything that matters really changed?

The day continues and the truth prevails. Mordecai is honored while Haman is humiliated, indicted, and hanged. What more could one day hold? It was just one day earlier that deliverance for the Jews had appeared hopeless. Who would have thought that the one who threatened their lives would be the one to die?

We need to be reminded that God is not subject to our timetable. Even though we may not see his justice in our lifetime, his justice guarantees that all unfairness will be dealt with. Biblical history proves that God is consistent in his justice and that all things work together for good for those who love God.[1]

Revelations

Esther revealed her nationality as a Jewess (7:3, 4). She then revealed that Mordecai was her cousin (8:1). There was nothing to hide. For the first time in five years, her heritage and her relationship to Mordecai could be common knowledge in the palace and in the empire.

1. Read Esther 8:1–6. As compensation for the wrong against her and her people, what did Ahasuerus give to Esther (v. 1)?

2. What did the king transfer to Mordecai, and what did this symbolize (v. 2)?

What a work of God's hand! At the Jews' darkest hour, He installed both a Jewish queen and a Jewish prime minister in Persia. Not only were Haman's possessions given to the Jews, but his position, responsibilities, and authority were also transferred to those from whom he had tried to take everything.

The ironies continue:
- Haman's injured pride had driven him to plot the destruction of Mordecai and the Jews; the king's injured pride had driven him to execute Haman. . . .
- Haman's plot to destroy Mordecai leads to Mordecai's acquiring both Haman's position and property."[2]

If this story were only about the lives of Esther, Mordecai, and Haman, there is the temptation to celebrate the downfall of the evil and the reward given to the righteous. But Esther emphasized to the king that the future of the Jewish people was still at stake. Esther's burden for her people remained her consuming motivation, greater than any other concern in her life.

3. How did Esther appeal to the king a second time (v. 3)?

4. How did the king respond to this display of emotion by his queen (v. 4)?

5. What did Esther ask the king to do (vv. 5, 6)?

A New Order in the Kingdom

Although Haman had been executed and was no longer a personal threat, the situation of impending doom for the Jews because of the decree issued during his tenure in office did not change. The original decree that legalized their annihilation could not be annulled. The Jewish people had already been aware of the decree for more than two months. Eight months remained before the scheduled day of execution.

6. Read Esther 8:7 and 8. Who originated the idea of a new decree (vv. 7, 8)?

Even though the first decree could not be altered, a second one was written in every language for each province. "The very purpose of this [second] decree was to counteract the first decree point by point (cf. 3:13) so that the Jews would not be left to any disadvantage at the hands of their enemies."[3]

The second decree from Shushan concerning Esther's people was distributed to the provinces in the same manner as the first one was. Time was short; within eight months, each of the one hundred million people in the empire, fifteen million of whom were Jews, needed to be aware of the second decree.

7. Read Esther 8:9–12.

(a) Who composed the new decree (v. 9)?

(b) Whose authority was invested in this new decree (v. 10)?

(c) How was the new decree spread (vv. 10, 14)?

(d) What did the new decree permit (v. 11)?

(e) Where did this new decree apply (vv. 9, 13)?

(f) When were the provisions of this decree to be enacted (vv. 11, 12)?

Now the Jews had permission to defend themselves against those who might attack them first. The same government that demanded their execution now provided for their self-defense. The king let it be known that he was on their side, protecting and intending to preserve them. This new decree brought salvation and deliverance to people who would have perished otherwise.

Make It Personal

God has made two decrees for mankind. The first is one of doom; the second is one of salvation. His first decree states that **sin must be punished by death.**

8. How is this decree confirmed in the following verses?

(a) Ezekiel 18:20

(b) Romans 6:23

God has never canceled nor altered this decree, but through the person of Jesus Christ, God issued a second decree. It states that **there is a way to be reconciled to God.**

9. According to the following verses, how is this decree confirmed?

(a) John 3:16

(b) Acts 16:31

God has provided a Savior, a means of salvation. Acceptance of that Savior, Jesus Christ, gives life, hope, escape, and much more. It is the only way to be released from the doom and death of the first decree. "A Savior is provided. All who avail themselves of God's gracious interference are saved. All who reject the means of His providing, do so at their own peril."[4]

We have good news that needs to be shared today. Just as the people living in Persia needed to be aware of the second decree, so do people today need to know of God's second decree. Only when they know of His saving grace through the Lord Jesus Christ can their impending doom be averted. "God's death sentence hangs over a sinful humanity, but He has also commanded us to hasten the message of salvation to every land."[5]

10. Whom do you know who is hopeless and in need of a Savior? With whom will you share the news of God's second decree?

New Standing for Esther's People

The decree written by Mordecai provided a means of salvation that the Jews could accept or reject as they chose. Those who did not believe the second decree remained hopeless, but those who placed confidence in the word of the king and believed the decree had great hope for deliverance. The Jews had been hurt deeply by the first decree; they could rejoice greatly in the salvation made possible through the second decree.

The first decree was made to destroy them by death; the second one was made to save them with life. The first one produced sorrow, and the second one produced joy. How exciting it is as a reader to watch "the resilient Jews quickly bounce from despair to hope."[6]

11. Compare Mordecai's clothing after each decree was issued (4:1, 2; 8:15). What did the changes symbolize?

12. According to Esther 8:16 and 17, what personal gifts or blessings did the Jews receive as a response to the new decree?

This reaction stands in marked contrast to the Jews' response to the first decree (4:3). What an exciting and extreme change there was from the mourning, fasting, weeping, and wailing of that day!

Make It Personal

13. Recall your response at the time you believed on Jesus Christ as your Savior from sin. What spiritual blessings have you received in response to salvation?

Can you see the hand of God continuing at work in your life? His sovereignty guarantees that He is always in control. He does not ever fail; He always makes a way of deliverance for His people.

We may experience frustration when life seems unfair, when the unjust seem to be prospering. We may struggle when God's justice seems to be slow in coming. Yet we can ask Him to help us trust Him with the big picture and to have patience with His timing.

14. What situation do you need to entrust to God and wait for His justice to prevail?

Notes

1. Max Lucado, *Life Lessons from the Inspired Word of God: Books of Ruth and Esther* (Nashville: W Publishing Group, 1996), 113. Used by permission of Thomas Nelson, Inc.

2. Jobes, 177

3. Whitcomb, 105.

4. H. A. Ironside, *Notes on the Books of Ezra, Nehemiah & Esther* (Neptune, NJ: Loizeaux Brothers, 1905), 92.

5. Whitcomb, 107.

6. Jeanette Lockerbie, *Esther: Queen at the Crossroads* (Chicago: Moody Press, 1974), 83.

11

From Fighting to Feasting— Let's Celebrate!

ESTHER 9; 10

"The LORD brings the counsel of the nations to nothing; He makes the plans of the peoples of no effect. The counsel of the LORD stands forever, the plans of His heart to all generations. Blessed is the nation whose God is the LORD, the people He has chosen as His own inheritance" (Psalm 33:10–12).

I CAN'T imagine preparing for a one-day war. I can't imagine the dread and fear that would consume all my energy during the countdown to that day on my calendar. I can't imagine that the good news in my life is that my loved ones and I will have an opportunity to defend ourselves. Can I really be sure this is good news?

Almost nine months passed after the events of Esther chapter 8. The good news of a second decree was spread throughout the Persian Empire, and the Jews prepared to defend themselves. Still, Haman's sons and other enemies of the Jews prepared to attack.

Self-Defense

1. Review Esther 8:7–14, then read 9:1–4. What did the Jews do in

response to the decree authorized by King Ahasuerus and composed by Mordecai (9:1, 2)?

2. What was the motivation of the Persian officials for aiding the Jews (9:2, 3)?

3. Read Esther 9:5–10. What was the outcome when the Jews defended themselves?

The day chosen by the "pur" as the day of Jewish destruction arrived. Instead of being a day of defeat, it was a day of great hope and deliverance. Even the Persian government officials aided the Jews in their self-defense.

According to Esther 8:17 and 9:2, fear of the Jews had fallen on the Gentiles. Many Gentiles sided with the Jews and acted as though they were Jews. Many of them accepted Judaism as their religion. Perhaps the Persians realized that "the God of the Jews was ruling over their destiny in a peculiar way."[1]

The number of dead is confirmation that many enemies had intended to take advantage of Haman's deceptively acquired decree that permitted Gentiles to attack the Jews (Esther 3). The Jews responded in self-defense against those men who attacked them, but they did not take any plunder from those whom they defeated (9:10).

A Lingering Concern

4. Read Esther 9:11–16. The king's interest in the actions generated by the two decrees is obvious in verse 12. What concerns did he voice to Queen Esther (v. 12)?

5. What were Esther's requests (vv. 12, 13)?

The granting of a second day for the Jews to defend themselves may have been due to knowledge of a plot. Perhaps Esther received word that additional enemies were planning to attack the Jews on the next day—at a time when the Jews would not legally be permitted to defend themselves. The hanging of Haman's sons would have deterred some Persians from attacking, but there were another three hundred enemies in Shushan, as well as seventy-five thousand in other parts of the empire, who did attempt to pursue Haman's goal (vv. 15, 16).

Similar outcomes were reported throughout the kingdom (v. 16). The writer who chronicled these things took care to mention three times that the Jews did not claim the plunder of their enemies (vv. 10, 15, 16), an entirely different behavior from what Haman had proposed for himself with his decree (3:13).

6. Read Genesis 12:3 and 27:29 and Exodus 23:22. How were God's promises proven true in Esther 9?

God delivered His people once again! He provided the way for deliverance without being seen or recognized and without having His name spoken. He was faithful to His promises and protected His people through His own providential care. Only He could orchestrate peoples, events, and situations.

Don't you long to hear God praised for His faithfulness and sovereign control in the lives of Esther, Mordecai, and their people? But even at the end of the book He is not mentioned. After being preserved by His loving hand, the Jews still offered no acknowledgment that it was the God of their fathers Who providentially delivered them.

Make It Personal

7. What is a part of your life for which you need to praise God and acknowledge that His hand directed and delivered you?

Consider sharing this life event with someone else, especially your children, grandchildren, or other relatives so they can recognize God's hand in your life and preserve the memory of His deliverance.

The Celebrating Begins

8. Read Esther 9:17—10:3.

(a) The Jews outside the city celebrated on the _____ day of Adar (v. 17).

(b) The Jews within the city of Shushan celebrated on the _____ day (v. 18).

9. How did they celebrate (vv. 17–19)?

10. What did Mordecai write to the Jews (v. 20)?

11. What did he want them to establish as a custom (vv. 21–23)?

12. What official position did Mordecai attain in the land of Persia (10:3; see also 8:15)?

13. The deliverance of the Jewish people from the plot of Haman is still celebrated today.

(a) What is this celebration called (9:26)?

(b) Why is it so named (3:7; 9:26)?

As prime minister of Persia, Mordecai assumed the responsibilities of protecting his people and of preserving the memory of their deliverance. He wrote letters that recorded the events, and he sent word to all the provinces that Adar 14 and 15 would be observed annually as a reminder of the day when the Jewish people were preserved. What a turn of events to be recorded!

These days of the Feast of Purim are days of celebration. They are days of feasting, giving gifts, and remembering the story of Esther. As part of the Feast of Purim, the book of Esther is read aloud. Every time the reader comes to the name of Haman in the text, the reader pauses. During this pause, the audience spits and makes derogatory noises. The synagogue reader is also careful to read the names of Haman's sons all in one breath because they all died together.

Even though Israel celebrates its physical and national deliverance, the nation and its people still lack a holy acknowledgment of God's faithfulness and personal work of deliverance. For the most part the celebration is reduced to an expression of patriotic, nationalistic gratitude.

Make It Personal

14. Read Romans 10:1–3. Take a few minutes to pray for the Jewish people. Ask God to lead them to righteousness through the blood of Jesus Christ.

15. As the Body of Christ, what celebration do Christians observe today in contrast to Purim? (Look at Mark 11:12–26 and 1 Corinthians 11:23–32 if you need some help.)

16. How does this observance celebrate deliverance for a follower of Jesus Christ?

The book of Esther stands as a lesson of how God works out His purposes through people who think they are working out their own. He works out His deep designs through people whom He has raised up; they do not even have to be aware of His hand in their lives.

Those who know the Son of God as personal Savior know that there is safety in God's sovereign hand. His purpose steadily advances, and it is awesome to realize that God chooses to use humankind in the accomplishment of His work. Truly the book of Esther stands as a lesson of providence.

Make It Personal

17. Enumerate some of the things you have learned about God and about yourself, as well as personal thoughts and attitudes that have changed, as a result of doing this study.

•

•

-

-

-

-

Notes
   1. Gray, 209.

LEADER'S GUIDE

Suggestions for Leaders

The effectiveness of a group Bible study usually depends on two things: (1) the leader herself; and (2) the ladies' commitment to prepare beforehand and to interact during the study. You cannot totally control the second factor, but you have total control over the first one. These brief suggestions will help you be an effective Bible study leader.

You will want to prepare each lesson a week in advance. During the week, read supplemental material and look for illustrations in the everyday events of your life as well as in the lives of others.

Encourage the ladies in the Bible study to complete each lesson before the meeting itself. This preparation will make the discussion more interesting. You can suggest that ladies answer two or three questions a day as part of their daily Bible reading time rather than trying to do the entire lesson at one sitting.

You may also want to encourage the ladies to memorize the key verse for each lesson. (This is the verse that is printed in italics at the start of each lesson.) If possible, print the verses on 3" x 5" cards to distribute each week. If you cannot do this, suggest that the ladies make their own cards and keep them in a prominent place throughout the week.

The physical setting in which you meet will have some bearing on the study itself. An informal circle of chairs, chairs around a table, someone's living room or family room—these types of settings encourage people to relax and participate. In addition to an informal setting, create an atmosphere in which ladies feel free to participate and be themselves.

During the discussion time, here are a few things to observe.

• Don't do all the talking. This study is not designed to be a lecture.

• Encourage discussion on each question by adding ideas and questions.

• Don't discuss controversial issues that will divide the group. (Differences of opinion are healthy; divisions are not.)

• Don't allow one lady to dominate the discussion. Use statements such as these to draw others into the study: "Let's hear from someone on this side of the room" (the side opposite the dominant talker); "Let's hear from someone who has not shared yet today."

• Stay on the subject. The tendency toward tangents is always possible in a discussion. One of your responsibilities as the leader is to keep the group on track.

• Don't get bogged down on a question that interests only one person.

You may want to use the last fifteen minutes of the scheduled time for prayer. If you have a large group of ladies, divide into smaller groups for prayer. You could call this the "Share and Care Time."

If you have a morning Bible study, encourage the ladies to go out for lunch with someone else from time to time. This is a good way to get acquainted with new ladies. Occasionally you could plan a time when ladies bring their own lunches or salads to share and eat together. These things help promote fellowship and friendship in the group.

The formats that follow are suggestions only. You can plan your own format, use one of these, or adapt one of these to your needs.

2-hour Bible Study

10:00—10:15 Coffee and fellowship time

10:15—10:30 Get-acquainted time

Have two ladies take five minutes each to tell something about themselves and their families.

Also use this time to make announcements and, if appropriate, take an offering for the baby-sitters.

10:30—11:45 Bible study

Leader guides discussion of the questions in the day's lesson.

11:45—12:00 Prayer time

2-hour Bible Study

10:00—10:45 Bible lesson

Leader teaches a lesson on the content of the material. No discussion during this time.

10:45—11:00 Coffee and fellowship

11:00—11:45 Discussion time

Divide into small groups with an appointed leader for each group. Discuss the questions in the day's lesson.

11:45—12:00 Prayer time

1½-hour Bible Study

10:00—10:30 Bible study

Leader guides discussion of half the questions in the day's lesson.

10:30—10:45 Coffee and fellowship

10:45—11:15 Bible study

Leader continues discussion of the questions in the day's lesson.

11:15—11:30 Prayer time

Answers are provided for Bible study questions. "Personal answer" questions are not usually provided.

LESSON 1: GOD RULES—EVEN IN DARKNESS

Notes for discussion leader

• Consider using "What a Mighty God We Serve" as a theme chorus for this study.

• Consider reading the entire book of Esther aloud together as your first lesson. You might have the ladies each read the part of a different character, using the script provided in the front of this book.

• Work through this lesson together. Affirm the lack of any such factor as "luck" in our lives. Ask ladies to share examples from their own lives about something that appeared to be coincidental but actually was the work of God. Remind them that we can be sure God is at work even when He appears to be least visible.

• You may be interested in using a contemporary short story that illustrates the lesson of providence. "The Sparrow at Starbucks," written by John Thomas Oaks, can be located on the Internet at http://www.christianitytoday.com/tc/2001/006/1.11.html[1]

Answers

1. The following answers are offered as examples of circumstances that evidence God's control:

• The king called for Vashti to display her beauty; this kind of request of a queen was unheard of in Persia.

• Queen Vashti refused to obey the king's summons.

• The king and his advisers overreacted and deposed Queen Vashti.

• A kingdom-wide search was made for a new queen.

• Esther was quite attractive physically.

• Hegai, the servant responsible for the king's harem, was partial toward Esther.

• Esther's heritage was unknown.

• The king chose Esther as his queen.

• Mordecai learned of a plot to kill the king.

• Mordecai's deed of foiling a murder plot was recorded but not rewarded.

• Haman was elevated with great authority.

• The date for execution of the Jews was eleven months after the date of the decree.

• Mordecai had access to the deadly decree.

• The king was not told that the decree was against the Jews.

• The king extended the scepter to Esther when she approached him uninvited.

• Esther decided to hold a second banquet before asking her petition; the king co-operated.

• Haman didn't find out about Esther's heritage.

• Haman prepared the gallows.

• King Ahasuerus had insomnia.

• The record of Mordecai's deed was read to the king.

• Haman was available to give counsel to the king as to how someone should be honored.

2. (a) Fasting occurs in Esther 4:3; after hearing of the decree, the Jews throughout the province fasted because of the deadly decree. (b) It also occurs in 4:16; when Esther made the decision to approach the king, the Jews in Shushan fasted on Esther's behalf.

3. Five feasts were held as celebrations: (a) 1:3: the king held a weeklong feast to show his might and to launch a military campaign. (b) 1:9: Queen Vashti entertained the wives of the officials with a feast. (c) 2:18: the feast of Esther, given by the king as a wedding reception. (d) 5:5: Esther held a private banquet for the king and Haman. (e) 7:1 and 2: Esther held a second private banquet at which she accused Haman.

4. Other likely questions: Why didn't Mordecai want Esther to reveal that she was a Jew? Was Esther's involvement in the beauty contest voluntary or involuntary? Did Esther's maids fast with her, or did they have any understanding of what she was doing? How does the story of Esther fit into God's permissive will as opposed to His perfect will?

LESSON 2: PUNISHED WITHOUT PARDON

Notes for discussion leader

• Consider reading chapter 1 aloud again.

• Vashti is not mentioned elsewhere in Scripture. It is not necessary to spend much time on the appropriateness of her response. Question 6 is intended to help the ladies make application to their own lives.

• Remind the ladies that God's providence is key; we see Vashti deposed as part of God's plan for using Esther as queen.

• Be sensitive to ladies who find themselves in very difficult situations, but take care that this does not monopolize your time together. Focus on the positive admonitions of the Scripture passages in question 7. Guide ladies to think of responsible actions toward difficult men.

Answers

1. He had called his leaders together for meetings that went on for six months.

2. Drinking.

3. She made a feast for the women in the royal palace.

4. He summoned the queen to come and display herself before her husband's advisors and officials.

5. She refused the summons.

7. (b) Live as a godly example; be faithful to God; pursue peace and Biblical wisdom; avoid petty quarrels; act with kindness.

10. Example answers may include compromise on the job when asked to do something contrary to policy, or the temptation to gossip within extended family. Many other answers are possible.

11. The goal is to be willing to pay any price. Often the hardest prices include loss of job or relationships.

12. Vashti would not appear before the king again, and her position would be given to another. Also, each man should be master in his own house and speak in the language of his own people.

13. The men feared that their wives would follow Vashti's example and defy their husbands.

14. The men intended that their wives would honor them as masters of their homes. (Without such an extreme decree, there would not have been opportunity for Esther to become queen.)

16. In my life (the writer), I want to be an example of God's standards of morality and proper conduct before my husband and children as well as to my extended family and to the ladies and girls of my local church and the college students and neighbors who cross my path.

17. God's counsel is to hold fast to faith in the Lord and to trust Him to be faithful no matter how desperate the situation.

LESSON 3: A SEARCH FOR A STAR

Notes for discussion leader

• Perhaps some of the ladies have seen the story of Esther in a glamorized, romantic way. Suggest that they discard that perspective and try to see the horror of the physical situation. Esther lived in an unfair society, one in which power was abused and the intervention of God seemed absent. Perhaps that is the situation of some of the ladies involved in this study as well. Ask for some examples of contemporary situations in which God does not seem present and those in leadership are abusing power for their own satisfaction.

• A concubine is a woman who came as a virgin to the king's bed and then lived in luxurious desolation in his harem. Some kings had hundreds of concubines.

• Encourage ladies to see God in their daily lives, even when an incident cannot be proven as connected to Him.

• Ezra and Nehemiah were used by God to reconstruct the temple, the walls of Jerusalem, and the spiritual condition of the Jewish people after their return from captivity. Ezra returned to Jerusalem from Babylon; he brought a remnant of the people to rebuild the temple. Nehemiah returned to Jerusalem from Shushan; he brought a remnant of the people to restore the gates and the city walls.

Answers

1. (a) From the king's advisors. (b) The plan was a compulsory beauty contest among young women selected throughout the kingdom; the king would be the sole judge.

2. (a) Mordecai, living in Shushan, the capital city. (b) His father had been carried into captivity when Jerusalem was captured by Nebuchadnezzar. Mordecai had grown up in exile from Israel. (c) Hadassah, also known as Esther. (d) Mordecai was her cousin; their fathers were brothers. (e) Shushan, the capital. (f) She was selected for consideration as a possible new queen and was moved into the king's palace in the care of the king's custodian of the women.

3. She would have at least been familiar with what the city was like; many young women from other parts of the empire had no knowledge of Shushan. And she had a close relative near at hand in the same city.

4. Answers will vary. Emphasize the fact that in most cases in which we recall feeling abandoned, we can look back and see God's hand. What a blessing to know that we were not really forgotten at all. I recall some times in which I could only anticipate hurt feelings, pain, and broken relationships from a situation. It was difficult to see beyond the pain to God's plan of strengthened relationships, protected futures, and hope.

6. Daniel. (You may wish to compare the religious commitment of Daniel and the account of a seemingly irreligious Esther. Daniel refused the king's food and voiced protest of Nebuchadnezzar's decree. Daniel participated in private prayer [6:10] as well as public praise of God after his deliverance [6:22–27]. Esther gives no indication of personal separation from the food or customs of Persia nor of a relationship with God.)

7. They probably had settled into a familiar, comfortable lifestyle. They did have some freedoms to marry and to own homes and businesses. To give up a settled life in order to return to land that had been left desolate would have required sacrifice.

8. (a) Provisions beyond the regular allowance; exceptional quality servants; the choice place in the house of the women. (b) She did not reveal her people or family, that she was a Jew or that Mordecai was a relative; Mordecai instructed her to keep that information secret. (c) Mordecai had access to the palace campus and could obtain news of Esther.

9. Invite volunteers to share their prayers of thanksgiving.

10. Answers will vary. A couple of ladies may be willing to share how God is working in their lives.

LESSON 4: ONLY GOD . . . CHOOSES A STAR

Notes for discussion leader

• We do not have any reason to think that Esther wanted to be queen. In fact, the text does not mention anything about what she might have felt about the situation. Because of her Jewish heritage, we must think that the possibility of intermarriage with an unbelieving Persian was seen as abhorrent.

Answers

1. (a) Twelve months. (b) Beauty preparations of oil treatments, perfumes, jewels, maids, and the personal attention of a beauty consultant. (c) After her night with the king, the young woman would be moved to live in the house of the concubines. (d) The king would call for her by name.

2. Esther was an orphan, reared by her cousin, Mordecai. She was very attractive physically, and she must have had a pleasing personality to win the favor of Hegai. She was submissive to Mordecai, her guardian, and she obeyed his direction not to reveal her Jewish heritage and family background. Esther was also submissive to Hegai, trusting his judgment and not asking for additional makeup and jewels to decorate herself. She must have been a very sweet, modest, and pleasant woman, beautiful in every way.

3. She chose to use only the ornamentation that Hegai advised. She did not take any gimmicks or extra adornment of makeup or jewels.

4. Esther won the king's favor. King Ahasuerus was more attracted to her than to any of the other women, and he made her his new queen.

5. Answers will vary. I (the writer) recall that when God was preparing to move us to a different ministry, He superintended details that seemed impossible. He caused other people to take over some of our responsibilities; He put missionaries on the field in record time; He brought in an amazing and unexpected amount of money to pay off a church building mortgage. In each case, these were not individual miracles, but they were clear demonstration of God's control over all of the things that touch our lives.

6. (a) Two doorkeepers plotted to kill the king. These were men who guarded the door of the king's private apartment or suite of rooms. These threats were not rare, and it was actually as a result of a plot similar to this one that Ahasuerus was assassinated in his bedroom in 465 BC.[2] (b) He got the information to Esther. (c) There must have been a trusted messenger. Any unauthorized man would have been forbidden to talk directly with Esther. (d) Esther sent the information to the king. (e) The information about an assassination plot against the king was investigated and found credible. The plotters were hanged. (f) The king might have been assassinated, which would have put Esther, as the queen, at great risk.

7. (a) Had the king not called for her and asked her to do something unacceptable, the king would not have become dissatisfied with her. (b) If Queen Vashti had not refused, she would have remained queen. (c) If the king and his advisers had not deposed Vashti, there would not have been a vacant seat for a new queen. (d) Only a kingdom-wide search for a new queen could open the door for a non-Persian woman to be considered. Otherwise, it was expected that the king would marry someone from one of the seven noble Persian families. (e) Only a beautiful woman would be selected by the king, but it was not required that she be from a family in the nobility. (f) Because Hegai probably was acquainted with the king's preferences, he gave preferential treatment to Esther. (g) As the queen, Esther would live in an influential position both with the king and within the empire. (h) Mordecai was able to show loyalty to the king and be noted as one to whom the king owed a favor. (i) Mordecai was the individual who received credit for saving the king's life. The fact that the deed was recorded foreshadowed its later recollection. (j) Because the reward was not given immediately, the postponement allowed for a favor to be paid at a later date.

LESSON 5: DEVISING DESTRUCTION

Notes for discussion leader

• When reviewing the story of the Amalekites found in Exodus 17, refer also to Deuteronomy 25:17–19. Haman was a descendant of the Amalekites. Due to disobedience in sparing Agag (1 Samuel 15:7–9), Saul (Israel's first king) was rejected by the Lord (v. 23). Samuel killed Agag (v. 33), but some of the Amalekites remained and returned to capture even David's family (1 Samuel 30:1–5). David killed all but four hundred.[3] The account of Haman in the book of Esther happened five hundred fifty years after the death of Agag.

• As you look at the person of Haman, think about the authority God has allowed you to have. How do you use it? Is it used to bring honor to God and help to others, or does it turn attention to you and fail to make Christ the priority?

Answers

1. In Esther 1:13 and 14 seven princes of Persia are named as the king's closest advisors. But in 3:1 Haman's name appears as "advanced above all the princes."

2. He was a vain son of an Agagite; he overreacted in anger because Mordecai would not bow; he became obsessed with a plot to destroy; he lied to the king; he was an enemy of the Jews.

3–4. Verse references for question 4 are shown in parentheses with the answers for question 3. A proud look (Esther 3:2). A lying tongue (3:8). Hands that shed innocent blood (3:13). A heart that devises wicked plans (3:6). Feet that run to evil (3:7). A false witness; one who speaks lies (3:8). One who sows discord (3:9).

5. Mordecai was introduced as a Jew of the tribe of Benjamin; Haman was introduced as an Agagite.

6. To kneel down and pay honor to Haman.

7. Mordecai refused to obey the king's dictate.

8. Haman was incensed and filled with wrath.

9. Do not ask ladies to share this answer; use this opportunity to remind ladies of the dangers of allowing hate to grow.

12. Haman's goal was to destroy the entire Jewish race.

13. Haman cast lots in order to gain direction from the Persian deities, astrologers, and magicians.

14. People make plans, but God controls them. He controls what people call "luck." Even though Haman cast the "pur" to determine a "favorable" date to annihilate the Jews, it was God Who controlled the outcome, not the deities of Persia.

15. He misrepresented the Jews as people who disobeyed the laws of the land.

16. He is described as the enemy of the Jews.

17. The order was to destroy, kill, and annihilate all Jews, both young and old, and children and women, on a certain day and to plunder their possessions.

18. Couriers carried copies to be published in all the provinces of the empire.

19. The citizens of Shushan were perplexed, bewildered, confused.

20. Answers will vary; encourage a couple of ladies to share their responses to this question.

LESSON 6: CHOOSING COMMITMENT WITH COURAGE
Answers

1. The Jews demonstrated their hopelessness with typical mourning: with fasting, weeping, wailing, and prostrating themselves in sackcloth and ashes.

2. He tore his clothes and went out into the city, wearing sackcloth and ashes and crying loudly, bitterly.

3. Hathach, one of the eunuchs who attended Esther.

4. We can assume that he was Jewish as well. Though his part in this story might seem unimportant, it actually was quite significant as he became the link in communications between Esther and Mordecai. He had to be thorough and accurate in each communication he carried, neither adding to nor subtracting from the messages he was given to deliver.

5. Mordecai communicated to Esther his belief that she should appeal to the king personally.

6. Esther was hesitant to approach the king because he had not called for her during the past month. She was not secure in her relationship with him.

7. Mordecai realized Providence must be at work in their lives. He saw this situation as a serious one demanding the personal risk of their own involvement.

8. (a) She was included in the decree. Being a resident of the palace would not allow her to escape death. Her life was in jeopardy either way. (b) Deliverance would come by another means. Mordecai evidenced confidence that Israel would not be annihilated.

(c) She was in a unique position to save her people. Her being in the palace was not an accident.

9. She was there to intercede for her people.

10. "Who knows whether you have come to the kingdom for such a time as this?" He communicated to Esther God's sovereign governing of His creation and people.

11. She communicated through the trusted servant, Hathach.

12. She asked Mordecai to gather the other Jews in the city and to get them to agree to fast together for three days and nights.

15. Human will is held in the hand of God. God is still in control.

16. Esther committed herself to approach the king (without being summoned), to identify herself as a Jewess, and to intercede for the lives of the Jewish people.

LESSON 7: TOO LATE TO TURN BACK
Notes for discussion leader
• Help ladies understand that Esther's decision to put her life at risk was the same decision that gave her the strength and courage to face the risks.

• As Esther approached the king, the threat of danger and the hope of life were equally present. Her defining moment was a life-and-death decision that went beyond her own life to touch the lives of others.

• Use this opportunity to present God's gift of salvation by grace.

• Haman's shallow, temporary happiness was dependent upon circumstances. If time permits, help the ladies recognize differences between temporary happiness and lasting joy.

• Haman's vanity and pride were clearly evident in his own house. Ladies should be encouraged to reflect upon the attitudes that are most prominent within their own homes.

• Haman is a case study in anger. Ladies should be cautioned about the dangerous effects of deep-seated anger.

Answers
1. (a) The king extended the scepter. (b) Esther touched it.

2. God controls the responses; man only thinks he is in full control. God was controlling the king's response to Esther's approach.

3. Answers will vary. You may want to include a presentation of the gospel at this point in the lesson.

4. Esther requested that the king and Haman attend a second banquet the next day. Note that the two people in Persia who can influence the king are together at each banquet.

5. Esther seems to have changed her mind. Readers would expect her to make her request immediately when she had gained the king's attention and favor.

7. (a) Haman was proud of his position and promotions as well as his invitations to the queen's banquets. (b) He called friends to come and hear his boasting.

8. Haman saw Mordecai, who did not show him any deference. Haman had a fixation for the destruction of Mordecai.

10. Haman's wife suggested that he eliminate the problem. He could do this by building a gallows seventy-five feet high for the purpose of hanging Mordecai. She indicated to him that getting rid of the problem (Mordecai) would allow Haman to enjoy the next day's feast.

(Ladies should be cautioned about the world's "solutions" to unwanted pregnancies, troubled marriages, and the inconvenience of elderly parents. Often the world's "solution" is to eliminate the problem for a moment without recognition of the greater costs that would result.)

LESSON 8: FROM SLEEPLESSNESS TO CELEBRATION
Answers

1. He had insomnia. This seems to be a coincidental circumstance, but it is actually a pivotal point in the book. (Ask the ladies to recall incidents in which their own lives were altered because they "just happened to" do or hear or read or see something.)

2. He asked to have the records (chronicles, annals) of his reign read to him. The written chronicles of Persia contained records of facts and events that were significant to the kingdom.

3. Ahasuerus realized that Mordecai had never been honored for revealing the threat to the king's life.

5. (a) The energy of his hatred motivated him to act at the earliest possible moment. He came to suggest that the king hang Mordecai on the gallows that Haman had prepared. (b) The king asked Haman for a suggestion of how he might honor someone, having Mordecai in mind, but the king did not inform Haman of whom he wished to reward. (Compare this to the lack of information that Haman gave to the king about the target of the decree in Esther 3:8.) (c) Haman suggested a royal robe, the king's horse with a crown, a public display. (d) He was convinced that he was to be the recipient.

6. The king instructed Haman to carry out his own suggestions—with Mordecai as the recipient of the honors.

7. Haman was compelled to publicly pay honor to the man he despised most. Even their clothes were reversed; Mordecai wore the clothes Haman had coveted instead of his own sackcloth and ashes, and Haman covered his head in mourning as soon as he could.

8. Mordecai went back to his job at the palace gate; Haman went right home. But Mordecai's honor did not change his status as a Jew; he still awaited execution.

9. God will bless those who bless Israel and will curse those who curse its people. Mordecai, a Jew, was experiencing God's blessing whether he acknowledged that or not.

10. Most likely he was fearful, uncertain, and aware that he was no longer in control.

11. Answers will vary. (a) God provides instruction, teaching, and guidance for His children. Seek those things earnestly. (b) God does have answers, and He will respond to our call. (c) God is unfailingly good; He is a trustworthy refuge for those in any trouble. (d) God desires that people believe on His Son and receive life in His name. (e) Our High Priest, Jesus (Hebrews 4:14), understands our weaknesses and knows how to overcome them; He offers a limitless supply of grace and mercy. (f) We can take great comfort in God's care; we can give our cares over to Him to carry for us.

LESSON 9: MORE SURPRISES AS THE DAY CONTINUES
Notes for discussion leader

• Help the ladies understand how quickly circumstances can be reversed. God is at work continually, even though we may not see the effects of His hand on our circumstances immediately.

Answers

1. (a) Esther asked the king to spare her own life and the lives of her people. (b) She told him that they had been sold for destruction, not merely enslavement.

2. She described him as an adversary and an enemy; she called him wicked (or vile).

3. Perhaps the king realized that his trust in Haman was gravely misplaced. Perhaps he suspected that Haman may have tried to manipulate him and misuse his authority in other matters. Perhaps he realized that he had signed a decree for Esther's death.

4. Haman pled with Esther for his life. He fell across her couch and knelt at her side.

5. No; Haman was charged with violence toward the queen. Inappropriate behavior toward the queen was punishable by immediate death.

6. The king commanded that Haman be hanged on the gallows.

7. Haman reaped his own death. The king became so angry toward him that he desired and ordered his death. Actually, Haman reaped all that he had directed toward Mordecai. (Caution the ladies to examine their own hearts; be careful not to allow pride, prejudice, or unforgiveness to energize or control actions.)

8. Answers will vary. (a) Pride will invariably bring trouble. (b) Uncontrolled anger is a mark of a fool. (c) Anger should not lead to sinful behavior. Anger should not be permitted to go unchecked. (d) Don't let yourself be motivated by personal ambition or pride. Instead, purpose to hold others in esteem.

9. (a) Haman's elevation to a place of authority contributed to his pride. Without his position, he would not have been the one to honor Mordecai or to attend Queen Esther's banquets. (b) Because the date for elimination of the Jewish race was yet months away, there was time for Esther to intercede and time for the Jews to work out another plan. (c) This gave credibility so that Mordecai's message to Esther was taken seriously rather than received as hearsay. (d) When the king extended his scepter, his consideration provided Esther the opportunity to intercede for her people. (e) This gave time for the king to be reminded of Mordecai's deed. It also gave time for more of Haman's duplicity to unfold. (f) Since Haman was not told that Esther was a Jew, he was not aware of a need to be careful. (g) Haman's pride and conceit caused him to be careless and to misread the significance and intent of Esther's banquet invitations. (h) Haman's passing Mordecai aroused his anger and caused him to complain at home so that his wife suggested building the gallows. (i) Though built for Mordecai, the gallows stood ready for Haman's own execution. (j) The king's insomnia gave opportunity for him to be reminded of Mordecai's deed on his behalf. (k) Haman's early arrival at the palace allowed him to be the advisor asked for counsel and to be placed in the position of giving honor to Mordecai.

LESSON 10: WAIT! WHAT ABOUT THE DECREE?

Notes for discussion leader

• There is great opportunity for a clear presentation of the gospel through this lesson. Leaders are encouraged to be prepared to explain God's decrees of doom and salvation. Stress the fact that God gave an alternative to death: Life in Christ.

• What a wonderful opportunity to see the gospel even in a book that does not mention

God's name. Don't let the ladies miss the great truth of God's grace and salvation.

Answers

1. The king gave to Esther all of Haman's possessions and his estate.

2. The king gave to Mordecai his own ring (the same one that signed the original decree). This symbolized his giving Haman's position, responsibilities, and authority to Mordecai.

3. Esther appealed to the king in a very emotional way.

4. He held the golden scepter out in acknowledgement and acceptance of her uninvited presence.

5. She asked him to revoke the decree devised by Haman.

6. The king proposed that Esther and Mordecai write a new decree; he gave them full freedom to write whatever they pleased. Again, the king took a passive role; he claimed to have done all he could.

7. (a) Mordecai. (b) The authority of King Ahasuerus. (c) By couriers. They rode swift royal horses and posted notices. (d) The new decree permitted the Jews to defend themselves by killing any who would assault them. (e) It applied to every province in the empire. (f) These provisions were to apply on the thirteenth day of the twelfth month, Adar, the date that Haman's "pur" had identified (3:7–13).

8. (a) The soul that sins will die. (b) The wages of sin is death.

9. (a) Whosoever believes in Jesus Christ should not perish but have everlasting life. (b) Believe on the Lord Jesus Christ and be saved (saved from judgment, punishment for sin).

11. Esther 4:1 and 2 state that Mordecai wore sackcloth and ashes, which symbolized grief, mourning, and sadness. In 8:15 he wore royal blue and white with linen and purple, which symbolized royalty, celebration, and rejoicing.

12. The Jews experienced the gifts of light, gladness, joy, and honor.

13. Answers will vary. Some suggestions are relief, peace, assurance of eternal life, privilege, song of joy, humbling, Friend, healing, new confidence, understanding.

LESSON 11: FROM FIGHTING TO FEASTING—LET'S CELEBRATE!

Notes for discussion leader

• The events of Esther 6—8 all happened on one day; note that eight months pass between chapter 8 and chapter 9.

• Be prepared to explain some parallels between the Jewish Feast of Purim and the Christian observance of the Lord's Table. Highlight the fact that both are celebrations of remembrance.

• Consider devoting an additional lesson to a mock observance of the Feast of Purim. Perhaps you could arrange for someone who works with Jewish people to conduct this for you. Among other resources, Web sites are also helpful.

> In the Synagogues and Temples, the Megillah, or Book of Esther, is read aloud. When the name of Haman, the Jews' enemy, is pronounced, children and adults alike, whistle, shake rattles, noisemakers, and

stomp their feet to blot out the name. The children have costume parties and the women bake "Hamantaschens," which are small pastries shaped like a three cornered hat (Haman's hat).

Even through [sic] Purim is a festive time, there is a period of fasting to remember that God heard His people when they fasted and cried out to Him. Also, Purim is a time for sending gifts of food to your friends and for helping the poor people in your community.[4]

Answers

1. The Jews gathered in the cities where they lived in Persia and effectively defended themselves.

2. They had fear of the Jews, and their support of the Jews put officials in favor with the king.

3. The Jews successfully defended themselves in Shushan; five hundred of their enemies died, plus the ten sons of Haman.

4. He wondered how Esther's people had fared in other parts of the empire. He also wondered what else Esther had on her mind; he sensed that she had another petition to make.

5. Esther asked that the same defense be allowed for another day for Jews in Shushan; she also asked that Haman's sons be hanged (they were already dead).

6. God protected His people; He proved to be an enemy to those who attacked the Jews.

7. Personal answers will vary. In my own life (the writer), God protected me throughout high school with His direction and provision for me to attend college.

8. (a) 14th. (b) 15th.

9. They celebrated with feasting, gladness, and joy. It was a holiday, and a time of giving presents.

10. Mordecai recorded the events and sent a letter.

11. He said that Adar 14 and 15 would be observed annually as a reminder of how a time of sorrow in their midst was turned to a time of joy.

12. He was elevated to the position of prime minister, second in the empire to the king. Mordecai was portrayed as great among the Jews and as one who sought their good and spoke peace.

13. (a) The celebration is called the Feast of Purim. (b) Because of the "pur" that was used to choose the date.

15. Born-again Christians observe the Lord's Table.

16. Christians remember the death, burial, and resurrection of Jesus Christ. We celebrate His freeing us from the bondage of sin and the impending separation from God as we would have been forever separated from Him.

17. Answers will vary. Some thoughts include the fact that Esther and Mordecai were not chosen and used by God based upon their own obedience and fidelity to Him, nor does He choose us upon any basis except His will. God's timing is perfect. God is in control even though we do not always recognize His presence or request His provision.

Notes

1. John Thomas Oaks, "The Sparrow at Starbucks" in *Christian Reader,* November/December 2001, Vol. 39, No. 6, p. 11. Referenced by permission of the author of www.oaksengine.com

2. Huey, 810.

3. John MacArthur, *The MacArthur Study Bible* (Nashville: Word Publishing, 1997), note on Exodus 17:14.

4. Leon Clymer, "The Feast of Purim," http://www.roshpinah.org/articles/Purim.html.